T0196039

Meant for More

Turning Passion into Purpose & Designing the Life You Were Made For

STEPHANIE HENDRICK

WESTBOW
PRESS®
A DIVISION OF THOMAS NELSON
& ZONDERVAN

Copyright © 2020 Stephanie Hendrick.

All rights reserved. No part of this book may be used or reproduced by any means, graphic, electronic, or mechanical, including photocopying, recording, taping or by any information storage retrieval system without the written permission of the author except in the case of brief quotations embodied in critical articles and reviews.

WestBow Press books may be ordered through booksellers or by contacting:

WestBow Press
A Division of Thomas Nelson & Zondervan
1663 Liberty Drive
Bloomington, IN 47403
www.westbowpress.com
844-714-3454

Because of the dynamic nature of the Internet, any web addresses or links contained in this book may have changed since publication and may no longer be valid. The views expressed in this work are solely those of the author and do not necessarily reflect the views of the publisher, and the publisher hereby disclaims any responsibility for them.

Any people depicted in stock imagery provided by Getty Images are models, and such images are being used for illustrative purposes only. Certain stock imagery © Getty Images.

Scriptures taken from the Holy Bible, New International Version®, NIV®. Copyright © 1973, 1978, 1984, 2011 by Biblica, Inc.™ Used by permission of Zondervan. All rights reserved worldwide. www.zondervan.com The "NIV" and "New International Version" are trademarks registered in the United States Patent and Trademark Office by Biblica, Inc.™

ISBN: 978-1-6642-0526-0 (sc)
ISBN: 978-1-6642-0525-3 (hc)
ISBN: 978-1-6642-0527-7 (e)

Library of Congress Control Number: 2020917521

Print information available on the last page.

WestBow Press rev. date: 10/21/2020

For my daughters, Dakota and McKenna.

Your dreams will always be worth chasing. Thank you for reminding me that simply encouraging you to pursue your dreams someday just isn't enough, and that I had to chase my own to show you it could be done.

Contents

Introduction

This is the part of the book you read while standing in the book aisle, shopping books by their covers, catchy titles and reading the first page or two- deciding whether the author has a message you want to hear. Arguably, it's the toughest section for an author to write. So, I'll cut to the chase for you with who I am and who I wrote this book for. *Spoiler alert: It's not for everyone.*

Having written most of this book from a local coffee shop while my two girls were in school, it feels appropriate to tell you that I'm a highly caffeinated, always-on-the-go mom of two little girls chasing purpose against a running clock. Amazon Prime is my sidekick and leftover, cold pizza makes my heart sing just as much as a 90's or 00's country anthem popping up on the radio. I've lived in Arizona most of my life and I can tell you firsthand that you don't get used to the heat in the summer. I'm married to the man that I knew was meant for me the moment we met *(Okay, okay, I stretched that truth a little. When we first met, I turned to my colleague and whispered, "If he has a younger brother, then I just found my husband." Turns out there was no younger brother.)* I'm the girl that built a massive sales team with her husband but couldn't find contentment amidst the success. I'm the girl navigating the God-given purpose despite not seeing the entire plan. And I'm the girl whose heart has a burden to reach a certain fraction of women.

> *Women that are ready for more in their life but don't necessarily know what that even looks like.*
> *Women who are ready for more but that feel it's a little too late or isn't the right season to lean into that big idea.*

Women who are ready for more but are convinced they don't have what it takes.

Maybe one of those last sentences made your stomach sink because you found yourself within one of them. It's okay if you did, friend. Most of us do.

Seeking purpose and pursuing that big idea can be more elaborate than the calculus equation your professor worked through over the course of an hour and a twenty-foot long whiteboard. The difference, though, is that you and I can't solve it through an equation. You won't finish this book with the entire thing mapped out. What you will have, however, is a new perspective on what you're truly capable of and a tangible way of attaining it step by step. Are you ready to see what you're made for?

You Are Meant for More

I'm going to ask you the same question I asked myself over and over the last few years. It's the question I couldn't answer as a child, as a teenager, as a college student, or even as a new parent. I avoided the question because digging deep was painful. Not painful because of a memory, but painful because I couldn't find an answer. I can rephrase this question a few ways, but you'll notice the overarching theme is the same. *What am I doing with my life? What am I actually capable of? Am I fulfilled?*

You were given a book of life with thousands of crisp, blank pages that are entirely yours to fill. The amount of detail on those pages is up to you. You hold the pen, and if you sit back and stare at the pages as they turn—blank page after blank page—nothing will be written until you put pen to paper. Yet the pages will still turn. Life is going by. If you're anything like me, the question "What am I doing with my life?" carries more weight the farther into the book you get.

You probably thought about this question in high school, and then again in college, but then the question became far less relevant after you graduated. You settled into a job and got your own place. The dreams and ambitions from your mid-twenties began to fade as the months went by. Your day-to-day decisions became less aligned with the life you envisioned for yourself and more aligned with your budget, your work schedule, and your metabolism (which, btw, decided to retire once you reached age thirty). Life became monotonous and pragmatic. Don't get me wrong—dating, planning a wedding, receiving a promotion, and buying a home are all milestones worth celebrating—but you might still feel as though something is missing. In the quiet moments when you're alone with your thoughts, you wonder what life could look like if only…

Sidelined by Seven in the Morning

I can remember getting in the car one Tuesday morning. The garage door opened, and a crisp breeze blew in. There's nothing like an Arizona morning in late October. The searing summer heat had subsided, and the cooler temperatures had begun to tease us a bit in the mornings. Our version of winter (because, yes, I realize that Phoenix doesn't exactly have a true winter) was within reach. The air softly grazed my cheek as I tried to open the back door without any free hands. Like most mornings, I was carrying McKenna's backpack while juggling a cup of coffee filled to the brim in the other hand and calling for her to come get into the car. With her sandy-brown hair parted into two braids and tiny frame somewhere beneath the hand-me-down navy uniform jumper, she walked into the garage a moment later.

"Look at my picture!" she said as she skipped toward me.

"Where are your shoes, Kenna?" I asked as she climbed into the car.

"I don't know. Did you see my picture?" she said. Maybe it's kindergarten life. Maybe it's that she's the baby of the family. Maybe it's that she takes after my husband. I'm not sure. All I know is that this carefree, playful little human reminds me daily that life is what you make of it. As I opened my own door, my oldest was walking around to her door, reciting her weekly poem that she would have to deliver in front of her fourth-grade class later that week. Dakota is a mini version of me- freckles across her nose, straight brown hair past her shoulders, and always focused on what's coming next.

Once we finally make it into the car, these rides to school are sometimes the absolute best part of my day. True, the morning is a frenzy. I can always count on having one kid who doesn't want to get out of bed, can't find their shoes, or is in complete meltdown mode over a missing headband. We repeat the same routine morning after morning. *Brush your teeth, brush your hair, eat something for breakfast (no, not the candy you just found in the back of the pantry), and go say bye to Daddy before we leave. You can't find your homework? The same shoes you wore yesterday don't fit anymore? Girls, it's 7 o'clock! Get in the car noooowwww!*

From there, though, things slow down a bit. I coast down our windy road, heading toward their school, knowing we have about twelve minutes together. We can listen to the radio, we can sit in silence, we can call "slug bugs," or we can just talk.

That Tuesday morning, we decided to talk. After I had casually flipped through six or seven radio stations all on commercial break at the same time, I turned the knob counterclockwise.

"Red slug bug! One point for me!" McKenna yelled. This is where I pause and explain to you that her sixth sense was finding any and every slug bug on the road. She loved them. Even more than the car itself, she loved finding them, calling them, and winning the game that only she was actually playing. She dreamed of the day when she could drive a white convertible slug bug.

"Good job, Kenna," I replied on autopilot.

"Mom," Dakota chimed in, "I still don't know what I want to be when I grow up. How did you and Dad know you were supposed to start your business?"

Kids' questions like this one always come out of nowhere, don't they? I was in the driver's seat, hair in a sloppy bun on top of my head, and a sip of coffee in my mouth. Yesterday's makeup was still on my face because let's be real- some nights, you're just lucky to make it into your own bed when you fall asleep. I didn't realize I needed to be boardroom prepared for this morning's drive to school. I'm often tempted to brush off the heavy questions—the ones that I know in my subconscious are questions I haven't answered fully for myself—from my girls, knowing that their questions have the ability to leave me unraveled long after the conversation has ended. On that particular morning, this innocent question highlighted the very issue that I wrestled with—it was a reminder that I'd pushed my own ambitions to the side years before. I'd taken the easiest route available to me and joined my husband's business.

Most of us moms don't end up pursuing the career that we proudly proclaimed at kindergarten graduation (and perhaps that's a good thing in some cases).

Did I admit to her that I'd just resigned myself to a business I was good at rather than pushing myself to build something of my own? That's God's honest truth.

I'd figured out something I was really good at (working in the mortgage industry), found a guy who did the same thing, married him, and we built a sales team together. It's a modern-day Cinderella story, I know. Were we successful at it? Yes. Did I relinquish my own dreams in order to pursue that career? Yes. And that's the part I was afraid to say aloud to Dakota.

Have you been there? Are you there right now? Did you put your own dreams up on a shelf and settle for what was most accommodating – or safer – at a certain point in time?

You're going through the motions day in and day out. You might be looking at the pages written in your own book, and they're uninspiring. They're safe. The story being told just doesn't light your soul on fire. Sound familiar?

Now let me acknowledge something you might be feeling—it's the reason you might not want to admit out loud that you even feel as though you settled into a comfort zone. You're afraid that this means you're not happy with the life you've created. You're afraid that this means you don't appreciate your current work (whether in the home, your own business, or for an employer). That isn't the case. You aren't ungrateful for your current blessings just because you admit that a small piece of you feels empty. You can be grateful for all that you have and still acknowledge that you're ready for growth.

I thought for a moment and then said to my daughter, "Honey, you can do absolutely anything you want in this life. That's the beauty of it all. You get to decide where to live, what to do, or who to serve."

Yes, that's right. I copped out and totally avoided her actual question. I do this often as a mom. Avoidance is my superpower.

"But did you always want to give people loans to buy their houses?"

She didn't let me avoid her initial question after all. *No, of course not,* I thought. There's a reason that mortgage lenders aren't an option in the Halloween aisle of Target. It's not glamorous.

"No, I didn't know this is what I would do when I was your age, honey. It's just how things ended up."

I pulled into the drop-off line at the girls' school and made my way through the parking lot. The girls quickly turned their attention to the kids arriving at the same time, eagerly planning what they'd do when they got to the playground. Dakota, the inquisitive mini version of myself in the backseat, had lost interest in her line of questioning for me, and she and her sister hopped out of the car and waved goodbye as they walked toward the double doors of their school. I waved back with a smile on my face and an uneasy feeling in the pit of my stomach.

I drove out of the parking lot and turned on to the very next street. I pulled over in front of the first house, put the car in park, and just cried. I cried because I was a fraud. I cried because I was thirty-two years old and knew in the depths of my soul that our two little girls wouldn't listen to what I said now or to what I would tell them in the years to come. I had just told them they could decide every aspect of their lives, but who was I kidding? Kids never listen to what we *tell* them. No, they do what they see us *do*. That's the truth, isn't it?

Here I was, telling them to chase their dreams and to become whoever it is that they dreamed of becoming. *Dream big, dream bold*, and I truly mean it when I say it to them. They're worthy of that ambition. I knew, though, that the same little girl who would pepper me with questions of my career choices would be the same young woman someday who would tell me it was okay for her to give up the fight because her mom had done the same thing.

I sat there, tears streaming down my face, and just let myself get lost in thought. I remembered my junior year of high school, walking into a huge classroom where all of our media classes were held. We had cameras, computers, and a small little "set" where we filmed the morning announcements for the rest of the school to see on the TVs in each classroom. We created funny little commercials to highlight a school dance or our team sports in season. We filmed, learned to edit our videos on the computer, and some of us got in front of the camera. That year, the teacher handed out a flyer that promoted a two-week camp for the Walter Cronkite School of Journalism at Arizona State University. No one around me seemed to really care much about what the teacher had handed out, but

I was ecstatic. If we had smartphones back then, I would have immediately sent a picture of it to my mom begging her to go. I knew I had to find a way. We would be staying in the college dorms. We'd be learning from one of the professors and working in the campus studio to get a feel for being in front of, and behind, the camera.

The flyer had instructions on how to apply for the two week program, as well as for how to apply for a scholarship. A scholarship was the only way I would be able to attend. That same night, I wrote a submission essay and asked my media teacher for a letter of recommendation so that I could apply. For the first time ever, I began to think about my future with a specific career in mind—an evening news TV anchor. A few weeks later, I received a letter in the mail that I had been selected to be in the program, and that I had been awarded the scholarship to cover my costs.

That camp was more than what I could have imagined. For two weeks, I soaked up every bit of what the professor taught us about how to research a story, how to film, how to edit our film, how to operate a camera, how to read from a teleprompter, and critiqued our news-style reporting. He spoke about a recent graduate who had just landed the anchor position on one of the major cable networks and how she'd sat and learned in the same seats we were sitting in.

We took a trip down to the leading news station at the time and sat behind the scenes during the evening news one day. It aired live, and we were allowed to watch the entire production from the back room. On commercial break, my professor called for me, motioning for me to come out into the hallway. He brought me on set to the lead TV anchor, a woman named Patti Kirkpatrick, who welcomed me and gave me a few encouraging words before the crew ushered me back out. It was a quick exchange, and one that I don't remember in much detail, other than the look on the other students' faces when I walked back into the room. They weren't entirely sure why I had been invited to meet Patti, nor was I, other than knowing I had expressed to our professor that I wanted to sit at the big desk someday like her.

My thoughts trailed off, and I wiped the tear from my left cheek. I was brought back to reality because the story doesn't go too much farther. While I had enrolled as a student at Arizona State University a year later, I'd graduated from their business school rather than the journalism school

I had taken the camp through. I resigned my dreams for the safety of a steady paycheck and benefits, rather than exploring what I could've done in the field of journalism. With journalism, I knew that I would have had to start in a smaller market somewhere and hope to work my way back to Arizona someday. I had succumbed to the uncertainty and chosen the safer route by avoiding the only career that had ever appealed to me in the first place.

Now, drenched in tears in the driver seat, I was a decade deep in a thriving mortgage business with my husband, yet I was wondering if I could somehow find a way out. Was it too late for me to change direction? Was I crazy to consider leaving when our business was doing so well? I felt like I'd already written too many pages into my own story to restart now. What would I even do? Why would I waste everything I had worked so hard to build with my husband? What would my husband even think—or say—to this crazy talk? I hadn't given myself the freedom to even think of what I'd want to do since my early college days. I no longer dreamed of reading the teleprompter on the evening news but knew that writing and speaking must have come naturally to me for a reason. God wouldn't waste a talent if it weren't going to be put to use, would He?

An Honest Moment

When you lose yourself in thought—I mean, really lose yourself—where do *you* see yourself? There is no one who gets to tell you what will work and what won't. You get to design your life. What does it look like if you allow yourself to envision a new thread in your story?

Take this journey with me: You wake up in the morning, where are you? What time is it? What's the first thing you do? Do you go for a run? Do you grab a cup of coffee and a book? Do you hop right into the shower? When you walk out the door, where are you headed? Are you on that drive to drop off kiddos, headed to the gym, or what job are you headed to? What does your morning look like? Are you around other people? Are you alone in a quiet office? What does the expression on your face look like? Are you laughing, smiling? Are you serious? How do you look as you move through your day? Do you sit up a little taller? Do you walk with confidence? Where are you in the afternoon? Are you stuck in traffic? Do you walk home? Are you at a sports practice or cooking dinner? Are you sitting around the family room playing a board game or binge-watching your favorite show with a close friend or spouse?

Take a moment to close your eyes and picture a version of your life that doesn't yet exist.

Life flies by—we all say that, and we all know what that feels like. We find ourselves in certain places, relationships, or jobs. And we let go of the pen. We set it down, and we let the pages flip, one after another, year after year. It's as if we hand the pen to someone else and let them continue writing the story for us. We stop trying to write out what we want to come next. We stop asking questions. The questions like, *what is my purpose? What am I actually capable of? If I'm not here in a year, what legacy—if any—am I leaving behind? Who did I inspire? Who did I serve?*

Take yourself back to your high school or college self. Yep, maybe you're back with bleach blond highlights, low-rise jeans, and a less-than-mediocre car. Let's go back to that girl, the one who wasn't yet knocked down by society's expectations of her. The one who believed she could live the life she dreamed of. The one who felt inspired to leave an imprint on this world. Some way, somehow. Think about how she felt, how she approached her future, how she saw opportunity. She had a vibrant spirit, big dreams, an adventurous side, and a plan for her future. As she grew, though, she started to conform to the workplace, to the opportunities that showed up soonest or easiest to her, to the safe route. The ambitions faded as the years went by, and she relinquished more control to what *came to be*, as opposed to designing what *could be*.

The idea of my own two little girls getting to this age and veering from their own passion breaks my heart. The size of their passion isn't what matters, the pursuit is. The income isn't what matters, the impact is. As a mom, there's no agenda to push them toward a powerful career as a C-level executive or an attorney, for example. The title isn't what matters, the passion behind it is. If one of my girls wants to become a teacher and settle in suburbia with a husband and 2.5 kids, I'm all for it. I will be incredibly proud of the difference they'll be making in their children's, spouse's, and students' lives. This isn't about titles, paychecks, or accolades. It's about knowing without a shadow of any doubt that it's exactly what they wanted, that it's exactly what they feel they were put on this earth for. That's the key—homing in on our purpose and relentlessly pursuing it.

Living a life of purpose and pursuing it not only fulfills you to your core, but it inspires others around you. It serves others around you and creates a ripple effect within our culture.

As a parent, we have this obligation to not only raise decent little humans, but to teach and inspire them to live a purposeful life. We sit back as they grow, and we comment to one another about their unique talents, what captivates their attention, and what stirs them up inside. We can begin to see their lives taking shape as they grow. We have a front-row seat to watching a beautiful story being written by our own children, yet we're often the ones who close the book on them. We're afraid of the failure or rejection that they may face. What we often fail to realize is that we keep them from success, from learning, and from impacting others when we close that book.

These kids, they're going to model their decisions based on what they witness, though. For little girls, Mom is who they think they're going to look like, act like, sound like, and be like when they grow up. I mean, it's how I knew that I was going to struggle with gray hairs at the front of my head. My mom gets them in that very spot, and I knew it was only a matter of time before I received my own slice of silver to take with me everywhere. My mom also worked harder than any woman I have ever known. She worked long hours, commuted an hour each way to and from work, and worked part-time jobs on the weekends to help pay for sports for my brother, sister, and me. She wasn't (and still isn't) a risk taker. As a daughter, I can honestly admit I don't remember any of life's lessons that she may have tried to teach me- verbally, that is- growing up. What I do remember is what I *saw* her do day after day. I learned strength and grit by witnessing it through the eyes of a child whose mother refused to accept defeat.

If I asked you to describe your mother, or any of the women in your life that raised you, what would you say? What words jump out at you when you picture that person? The words coming to mind are because of a specific memory, or maybe a compilation of memories, aren't they? Understanding that these memories shape your perspective of that person is what you need to keep at the forefront of your mind. *Your* actions become memories for those around you. Those memories ultimately become your legacy. What legacy do you want to leave behind?

Just as you can think back to your experience with your own mother, this is how I know that our words don't carry the weight that our actions do. Your mother or grandmother, aunt, or stepmother may approach life far differently than you do. There's the obvious reason—they came from a more restricted generation—but they were also each made with a unique purpose that we don't have to understand, just as they don't necessarily have to fully understand ours. Vastly different or not, I can certainly say that, though my mom has never been the type to take risks, had I not learned tenacity by watching her as I grew up, it would be far more complicated for me to pursue my own purpose. Can you see some of the interwoven threads, despite the differences between you and the women who raised you?

In the moment I found myself broken down in my car that Tuesday morning, I questioned the career decisions I'd made over the prior decade. A wave of responsibility weighed heavy on me in the driver's seat that morning. Whether I wanted it or not, every choice I made was going to create the storyline of who I was as "Mom" for our girls. With that daunting truth, I decided to leap blindly in the direction that was calling me.

It's Never Too Late to Seek Your Purpose

I don't care if you're thirty-three or fifty-three. It's never too late to look deep inside and seek purpose for your life. Purpose might be a clear objective for some of us from a young age, while others of us might be on more of a self-discovery journey. We might think we've homed in on exactly what we're here to do, only to see it change course the further we go along. Our purpose at one point in time could quite possibly look very different later. Does it mean the purpose has changed? Maybe. Does it mean the purpose is evolving, just as you are? Sounds pretty reasonable to me.

Not Quite What She Pictured

Oftentimes, we feel an urge pushing us in a certain direction, but we're afraid to follow through without having the idea solidified by someone else. Kind of like when your bestie reassured you that your outfit was on point in high school or gave you the skinny on the guy that asked you out in college. Validation is what we came to rely on and continue to seek.

Knowing this is how women often process their decisions, I invited a few girlfriends over one evening. There were four of us women sitting together in my living room sipping wine and opening up to one another. Aside from my sister-in-law, Andrea, we were all relatively new to meeting one another. Our kids were similar ages, we lived in the same neighborhood, and honestly, we just needed an excuse to let our husbands and kids fend for themselves for a couple of hours on a Tuesday evening.

As the conversation went on, we started talking about the idea that each of us was meant to seek purpose in our lives. I don't know if the wine got us there or not, but we found ourselves in one of those deep conversations where you really start to see the girl beneath the persona. As we each shared our thoughts and struggles with the idea, Andrea spoke up. She looked off to the side as she began to describe this tug on her heart to go on a mission trip. Our nearby church organized mission trips all over the world every year. She dreamed of the day she could go and serve people halfway around the world.

One of the women asked her why she didn't just sign up. She took a deep breath, a sigh really, as if to say that she'd already thought through this scenario time and time again. She explained that she and her husband didn't know if it was the right time for her to take such a big trip, a trip thousands of miles away and one that often lasted ten days or so. Their son was in kindergarten and being away from her family for that amount of time would be too much on her husband and son. You could tell by the way she spoke that she was reciting the narrative she had told herself.

Though I wanted to pull her aside and tell her to follow her instinct, to trust that her family would be fine, and to tell her not to ignore the urge to serve, I simply nodded and kept quiet. I could hear my husband's voice in my head. *Stephanie, don't push too hard. Maybe she's scared. Maybe it's a tough conversation for her and my brother. Let it be. Don't make family get-togethers weird.* Truth be told, Brandon's never actually said those words to me. Much like the narrative I suspect was in Andrea's head, I had made up my own as well as to why I shouldn't try to push a little harder with her.

About nine or ten months later, I found myself at her home for dinner one evening. The kids were swimming in the pool with our husbands, and she was inside pulling food out of the oven. She looked up as I walked toward the kitchen and asked her what she'd been up to lately. As she moved the hot pan from the oven to the stove to cool down, she said she wanted to show me what she'd been working on the last few weeks. As she tossed the oven mitts onto the counter, she ushered me into her spare bedroom right off the kitchen.

I followed her into the room and watched as she slid the closet door open. Inside the closet were plastic bins—labeled, organized and neatly stacked—with various things she was collecting for homeless veterans she explained. She had heard of an organization downtown that collected daily necessities (toiletries, socks, pillows and so forth) and distributed them to veterans in need. Andrea was an avid couponer and had tapped in to how to get ridiculous deals on things like pillows, toothbrushes and toothpaste, protein bars, socks—major essentials. As I looked at the different bins, each of them stuffed to the brim, she told me about the trip she had just made to the shelter a few days prior with over forty pillows she had found on clearance at a store. Her spirit was vibrant. She spoke with a smile, she looked me in the eye, and she proudly told me about how she had figured out a way to contribute far more than she'd ever imagined by watching for crazy coupon deals.

She slid the closet door closed and pointed toward the dresser drawers behind me. As I turned, she walked over and opened them one by one, showing me more supplies that she couldn't fit in the bins she'd just shown me in the closet. Astonished, I looked at her and said, "Do you remember that night we talked about our purpose last year?" She nodded. "You wanted a mission trip so badly, and you knew it was where you were being pulled. I think you were right. I think the part you just hadn't yet realized is that your mission field was right here. Look at all this stuff you've been able to find crazy deals on and then finding the veteran center that desperately needs this stuff. You didn't have to go halfway around the world."

Weeks later, she would text me a picture of an entire grocery cart full of cereal boxes. There must have been fifty boxes, and she'd snagged them for about twenty-five to forty cents per box. She was a completely different woman than I had seen months earlier.

A few months passed from that evening. Andrea was at my front door one Sunday afternoon, dropping off her son to play with our girls. "I'll be at home tackling the garage. There's so much stuff in there and I need to organize it onto some shelving." I knew (or so I thought) exactly what she was referring to and asked her why she was moving the shelter donation items from the spare bedroom and into the garage. "No, not that stuff" she said with a chuckle. She went on to explain that she'd begun chasing down clearance sales on all sorts of random items as she came across them and then reselling the items for small profits on online platforms. She then used those profits to purchase the items she knew she needed for the veterans' shelter. She had orchestrated an entire plan to fund the charitable cause to a larger scale than she'd first started with.

This is what it looks like to take the pen and start a new chapter in your life. Andrea had picked her pen back up, and she began writing the purpose-driven story she wanted to read.

The Sermon That Changed It All

As you know by now, I struggled with finding my own purpose. Maybe the more accurate admission is that I struggled to recognize it in the first place. I was sitting in a sermon one Sunday morning, holding my hot vanilla latte with nonfat milk and no foam (you know, just in case you wondered how I take my latte) in one hand, and the other hand resting on my husband's knee beside me. I was more engaged in this sermon compared to any other that I had heard in the prior ten years I'd been attending our church. I knew the sermon would be on seeking purpose and I was at the edge of my seat waiting to figure this out once and for all. I was listening to the pastor's every word, desperate for the words to resonate with me and create the *ah-ha* moment I had hoped for, for years.

Is he going to tell us how to find our purpose? Is God going to speak to me? Am I going to finally know what I am actually supposed to be doing? Inside, I was begging for answers and had been for a long time. The pastor walked us through an exercise to help open our minds to what many people probably felt was philosophical nonsense. He first had us reflect on what our skills and talents were. What had other people told us we were good at, for example? What strengths did we know that we had? These skills could be anything that we'd ever known about ourselves to be good at or been told by others.

I thought, *Well, I'm super organized. I make a system out of every aspect of my life to get a ton of stuff in a short amount of time.* Productivity. That had to count, right? There's a method to the day I do laundry, the day I order groceries online (and the mere fact that I order them online even)—just as much as there's a method to how my email inbox is organized into various folders.

My thoughts then veered away from productivity and focused on the time I had been asked to do a presentation at a prior employer. The owner had said I spoke and presented well and that I had a great way of teaching things. That had always stuck with me. *So, I'm able to stand in a room of strangers and speak well. Okay, there's a starting point,* I thought.

Before my thoughts could go much further, the pastor told us to set aside the talents we had just recounted and start thinking about what our passions were. He reminded us that passion was a strong emotion and didn't have to be a positive emotion. If something struck us and really made us upset or angry, that was still passion. A couple thoughts came to my mind. I'd once wanted to get my journalism degree. I loved writing, and I had also thought it would be amazing to be a TV news anchor. I wasn't shy in front of others. I even had the fashionable bob haircut of 2004, just like so many of the TV broadcasters at the time. I was emulating the part as if ABC or NBC was going to recruit me right out of my public high school. I mean, the CIA recruits straight out of high school, so why not major TV station producers, right? *Okay, so is this a passion then?* I began to doubt my thoughts. I was so confused. *Maybe you're not thinking of passions, Steph. Maybe you're just thinking of things you're drawn to. Writing. Speaking.* I wanted to raise my hand and tell the pastor I was confused and likely doing this all wrong. Given there were about 3,500 other people in the room quietly pondering their own passions, that wasn't an option, unfortunately.

I took a deep breath. *Okay, what about a passion of mine that maybe struck a different type of chord, though? What drives me crazy or upsets me?* My mind shifted to the life I was living in that moment. I was a mom, a wife, and a businesswoman. It wasn't the roles that bothered me. It was the cultural expectations that everyone placed on each of those roles. The colleagues who called me an assistant (because I was a woman) rather than an equal partner in my business with my husband. The generation that believed a wife and mother only had a place in the home. *Work-life balance. Mom guilt. Glass ceiling for females.* Sure, there were a few topics that could fire me up. The pastor pulled us back in from thought before I could get much further. "Where do those two intersect?" he asked. "You'll find purpose when you put your talents and your passions together."

The service wrapped up, and as my husband and I were walking out, we were both silent. We were lost in our thoughts, clearly trying to process the questions, the ideas, and how they might weave together.

Something happened in that service that I cannot fully articulate. It was the first time I'd been still enough to let the thoughts take over. I could hear suggestions in my mind that I'd never consciously been aware of before. *There's more that you're capable of,* I heard. *Most people are playing so much smaller than what they're capable of. There are more women like you. Women that find themselves raising kids and businesses. Women that think it has to be one or the other. You're not the only one that struggles to balance these two worlds.* I wanted to argue back that I'd wanted to know what I was meant for, what my purpose was, for years. I'd been asking and coming up empty for years. If I was meant to do more than what I was currently doing, then why hadn't it been abundantly clear all this time? The inner voice already knew my argument because the response was immediate. *You weren't ready.*

We were still walking along the sidewalk outside of the auditorium where service had just wrapped. Still walking hand-in-hand in silence, I looked up at my husband and said, "I'm going to start a blog." The words fell out without any conscious thought behind them. *Wait, what? Where did 'blog' come from?* I hadn't thought about a blog in those prior moments—or ever. What was I even going to write about? For the first time in my life, without a plan, I decided in that moment to lean in and to let go. From there, pursuing one step at a time, the blog led me right here to writing this book for you.

That's not where this story ends, though. This book isn't about me and my pursuit of purpose. My stories are here to illustrate the point and to guide you as you begin your own journey. This book is about sharing that pursuit and showing *you* how to do the same.

Chapter Takeaway

It's one thing to listen to a motivational speaker or read an inspiring book, but it's entirely another thing to implement the tools that you're being given. You can skim over the questions at the end of each chapter, but I can promise you that taking the time to think about the questions, write out your ideas, and refine your ideas later will allow you to build out the plan that you need in order to experience the transformation you are seeking.

With the questions below, write down anything and everything that comes to mind. There are no right or wrong answers.

These are the things *I've been told* are my strengths:

_____

_____

These are the things *I know* are my strengths:

_____

_____

The things that evoke the most emotion out of me (these are things you're passionate about, which can have both positive and negative emotions associated with them):

_____

The first thing that comes to mind as I read through my strengths and my passions is:

_____

(HINT: When you intertwine your strengths/skills and your passion, you begin to narrow in on what your purpose is. If it's not yet abundantly clear, that's okay! Remember, mine wasn't either.)

Who Am I to Think I Can Do This?

When my parents needed a sitter for my younger siblings and I, they would call the Conner family. The Conners had three daughters—Jen, Chrissy and Lori—and lived on the next street over from us. Jen and Lori were both cheerleaders and found it easy to entertain my younger sister and me by teaching us cheer routines or tumbling moves. They are also the sole reason I know New Kids on the Block songs and watched *90210*, but now we're getting slightly off topic.

In the front living room of our home, we learned cartwheels and choreography. We did handstands with our toes reaching up the wall just beneath the school pictures hanging in the entryway. With their spotting, we learned to backbends, back walkovers and eventually back handsprings. By the time we got our first trampoline in the backyard, needless to say, we were mastering back handsprings and flips on our own. We could recite the cheers at the Friday night football games from the stands (my dad would take us to the games so we could watch the Conner girls cheerlead) and loved any chance to learn a new cheer routine when one of them came to watch us.

Before long, my parents enrolled both my sister and me into gymnastics. The sport came natural to me, and I was quick to learn new skills. I loved that there was always a tougher skill to learn and to perfect. Within about a year, the coaches asked my parents for a meeting in the office (which I remember thinking was super odd). They offered me a spot on the "team" if my parents could commit to the practice schedule—and cost (hence, the reason there was a private meeting before the coaches could tell me I was ready for the "team"). My parents both found part-time jobs almost immediately.

Gymnastics, if you aren't terribly familiar with it, is a sport of extreme discipline. I can remember spending four hours a night—every single weekday—at the gym. That may sound excessive, but there are four rotations in any gymnastics competition—the uneven bars, the floor, the vault, and the balance beam. We would train on every rotation for an hour each practice. We were also required to take two or three hours of ballet and jazz classes in addition to our training schedule.

As nutty as that schedule sounds, I loved every moment of it. My teammates and coaches were my second family, and I was theirs. A few of my teammates and I carpooled to practices together. We'd do our homework in the car on the ride to and from the gym as we'd eat dinner from a lunchbox that our moms had packed us earlier that morning.

As I think back to those days, I can honestly tell you that there wasn't a thought in my mind that I would ever stop progressing in the sport. As children, we have the gift of blinders. Blinders for failure. Blinders for our own skill level. Blinders for fear. The blinders may be ignorance in the opinion of some, but ignorance from what? That we're unaware of what it means to actually fail? Unaware of how we compare to our teammates? Unaware of fear determining how far we can truly pursue something? If I could figure out how to create those blinders again, as an adult, I'd do it in a heartbeat.

As I mentioned earlier, I didn't know there would ever be a skill that would hinder my progress as a gymnast—until there was.

Four Feet Up and Blind

One day, my teammates and I were on beam rotation. Our coach told us we'd be learning to do a front handspring on the balance beam. Now, the skill itself wasn't new. We'd been doing front handsprings for quite a while on the floor. That afternoon, we were just taking the skill up about four feet in the air and in a straight line that was only four inches wide.

Like any new skill on the beam, we'd often practice it on a piece of white masking tape that was taped to the floor. We'd progress to a low beam, just a piece of covered wood that sat maybe six inches off the ground- enough to get used to hand and feet placement. From there, we'd move to another beam a couple feet off the ground and ultimately move to a standard high beam.

When we moved to the high beam, we'd place huge blue mats underneath so that if our footing slipped, we wouldn't fall four feet to the ground. We became comfortable on the high beam, and then the coaches would move the mat out from underneath it. They'd stand next to the beam, which was more for moral support, given that their head is about even with your kneecap, as you practiced over and over until, eventually, you were doing it on your own.

The front handspring terrified me. The skill itself was easy—I would do it in the grocery store aisle or in someone's driveway without thinking twice. Moving it up onto the high beam was a different story, though. I stood on the beam, my teammates on the beams to my right and left and my coach shouting, "Point your toes!" and "Good! Again!" in the background to my teammates. I stood there, in the same spot on the beam, for the majority of the hour that night. I was frozen in fear.

Our beam coach, Donna, was intimidating. Donna had super short, white hair and a stern voice. I don't know if I ever saw her crack a smile. She had very little patience, and she clearly had never had a fear in her life as far I knew. "Stephanie, what are you doing? Stop standing there. Let's go!"

My eyes welled with tears. The bottoms of my feet were sweating and leaving footprint marks on the top of the beam. I would put my hands up in the air, tight to my ears, and stand with my left foot pointed straight out in front of my right foot, as if I were about to attempt the skill. That inner voice began to set in. *You're going to miss the beam. You can't see where you're going, and you're going to fall. Your foot will slide right off the side of the beam, and you can smack your face on the beam as you crash land.* (My inner voice doesn't sugarcoat things.)

I didn't know how to reason with the voice. It was right. Unlike a back handspring, where you can see the beam before your hands and feet touch down, a front handspring was a blind skill. Your feet would touch the beam without your eyes on the landing strip. With any sort of front handspring or front flip, your eyes were the last to come up.

Alas, after Coach Donna came over and began challenging the voice in my head, I went for it. As intimidating as Coach Donna was, she knew what we were each capable of. She knew that the skill itself wasn't the hindrance, it was fear. With her countdown, "3, 2, 1," I began to lunge forward, arms straight up in the air next to my ears, my left foot in front. I pushed with my left leg as I put my hands on the beam and let my body follow the motion it had done so many times before.

I landed the front handspring and looked over at Donna. She still didn't crack a smile. "You were stressing over nothing. Keep doing it. Over and over. I want ten more before you get off this beam. Let's go," she said.

I had been capable of doing it the entire time, but I'd needed that push. At nine or ten years old, I didn't quite know how to push myself when fear got the best of me. I needed someone else to replace the voice of caution and failure, to reassure me that I had the skill, talent, and ability to do this. Eventually, my own inner voice—the confident, resilient one— replaced Donna's. It had to. I had to train the voice in my head to be the encouragement and nudge that I needed.

Which One Are You Listening To?

We all have that inner voice. Actually, we all have two inner voices. There's the inner voice that encourages you and the one that suppresses your ambitions. They're in a constant battle up there. We tend to listen more to the pessimist than the optimist, don't we? It takes focus and intention to control which voice narrates the majority of your life. I beg you to leave the volume turned up on the voice that encourages, challenges your fears and thoughts, and introduces ideas that never seemed possible. Don't drown out that noise. You need that noise. It's guiding you in the direction that you're meant to go. Just like Coach Donna for me in that moment on the high beam, the inner voice wants to tell us that we are far more capable than we could've ever imagined.

The other voice, though? That inner critic who reminds you of every insecurity, blemish, and fault that you have—don't ever let that voice rise to a level that keeps you from taking a step forward. Don't ever let her convince you that you don't have what it takes, that you lack the experience, that the dream is bigger than your abilities, or that you're making up your purpose in your head. That voice is full of it. That voice is incredibly difficult to turn the volume down on. It's persistent, and it will take intention for you to stop each and every time it begins to tear you down, and to rephrase those statements into affirmations instead.

You are worthy of the dreams in your head—the ones you're scared to say out loud, the ones that keep you up at night and give you butterflies in your stomach. Do you know how I know that those dreams are legitimate? I know because no dream is placed on your heart by mistake. The things that you're passionate about (whether it evokes a positive or negative emotion—passion is just a strong feeling toward something), the skills that you excel at, none of it is by mistake. In my opinion (and you can disagree if you'd like; we can still be friends), those are God-given gifts. You were created with a purpose.

Ever wondered why you're passionate about things that are different than your sister, your spouse, or your mom? It's because you were uniquely made with a specific purpose in mind. Knowing that purpose, He gave you certain abilities and desires in the hopes that you would stop long enough to listen to the purpose that your heart tries to whisper to your mind ever-so-quietly.

Trust Your Gut

What do hear when you are still? When things are quiet, and you're alone with your thoughts, where does your mind drift to? Do you start to feel as though you've *settled* in life? Listen closely. If you feel that something is missing, it's not something to be ashamed of. Please don't confuse that line of thinking with being ungrateful for your family, your job, your marriage, your kids, or your home. They are not related. Your job, your family, and your circumstances are undoubtedly part of the story. *Part of* the story. Not necessarily the *entire* story.

I can remember being twenty-three years old with a newborn. About six weeks into maternity leave, I sat on the couch in our family room with Brandon. Dakota was tightly wrapped in a swaddle blanket and asleep in my lap. "I don't want to go back. I don't want to put her in daycare," I said as I looked down at her. My eyes immediately welled with tears.

This was a loaded statement, and one that Brandon wasn't anticipating. We hadn't discussed me leaving my job up to this point. Our country was in the middle of a recession, Brandon's income was 100 percent commission-based, and I was asking to walk away from my salaried job. The very job that our health insurance came from. The very job that at least had a guaranteed paycheck every two weeks.

To my surprise, he agreed within minutes. Because of Brandon's demeanor in that moment and in the weeks that followed, the decision felt aligned with what I wanted. Months later, alone with my thoughts one afternoon, I sat on the landing of our staircase and cried. I didn't know why I was crying, exactly. I just knew that things didn't feel right. I knew that I had gotten exactly what I thought I'd wanted, but something felt as though it were missing.

Though it took me awhile to understand what was missing, the very idea of admitting this to myself—nonetheless to Brandon at some point—was shameful. I felt as though he'd see me as ungrateful for the work he was putting in so that I could leave my job and stay home. I harbored those feelings for weeks before I admitted them to him one day.

I prefaced the conversation by acknowledging my gratitude for his work, for our home, for the food in our pantry, and for the life we were creating. I was terrified to admit that I felt as though I had settled, and more so terrified that he would perceive that statement as meaning that I had settled with *him* or *our daughter*. That was not the case. That never became the case. The feeling of settlement was entirely within what I used my mind and skills for on a day-to-day basis. The feeling of settlement was directly tied to my desire for accomplishing something tangible, for contributing my thoughts and knowledge and seeing the impact I could make in the business world—the marketplace I had studied in college, obtained a degree for, and found a voice within over the prior few years.

The idea of having settled had nothing to do with becoming a mother. I was just afraid that others would perceive it that way if I openly admitted that I wanted to work—in some capacity—after giving the SAHM thing a try for a few months. Do you see the difference? You may even be able to relate to that specific feeling, but do you also see how it can be incredibly difficult to articulate this to someone? *Phew.* It's overwhelming just internalizing what you're going through within your own mind. The idea of telling someone what's on your heart can be terrifying, right?

I shared this story with you because I want you to understand that it is completely normal for you to feel something similar. I want you to know that the nudge within your soul isn't meant to create guilt around your current circumstances. No, it's just the nudge to slightly alter your direction if you've made a wrong turn or the nudge that you're now ready for the next step in your journey.

This purpose looks different for each and every one of us. You might be exactly where you should be or you might be facing the wrong direction. Purpose can happen in the home just as much as it can happen in the boardroom. There's no specific job description, place, timing, or qualification. In fact, the purpose you are meant for is something you are very likely not even fully qualified for right now. Don't worry, you will be with time and persistence, but it's important that you be reminded that just because you aren't fully equipped for something *right now* doesn't mean that you aren't on the path that will ultimately equip you.

I'll forewarn you, though, that when you feel a sense of purpose begin to pull you in a certain direction, the self-doubt will be right beside it. "Turn around. Play smaller," the voice will say. "You don't have what it takes." "It's too late for you." "You don't have time for this." Or, my favorite one, "This isn't your purpose. You just want it to be."

Air-slap the naysayer. It's wrong. You do have the time. You do have the ability. In fact, you're capable of more than you're even envisioning for yourself. You're capable of playing bigger. It's never too late to decide you're ready for the next chapter in life.

Oftentimes, the idea of attempting something bigger than ourselves is overwhelming. It's too vast of a journey for us to fully envision. Stop looking at the long road ahead of you. Look down about *six inches in front of your feet.* That right there is where I want you to go. One step forward.

We don't need to know where the path leads. We don't need to know what is going to happen or not happen. We don't need to know how long it will take. None of that matters. What matters is one step at a time. When you take one step, you find the second one.

Much like my ten-year-old self on the balance beam, I felt I needed to be able to see the beam the entire time. The skill doesn't allow for you to see the beam the entire time. It takes trust—in yourself—that you can go for it and your feet will find the landing. It takes trust that if your foot misses the beam and you fall to the ground that you'll be okay. If you're a type-A personality, this is really hard for you. I know because I'm part of that clan. I lost months trying to research the entire path—the path to pursue my passion, that is—and hadn't taken a single step. Releasing control (which is precisely what type A's don't want to do) is met with an immense amount of reluctance.

After realizing that all of the literature, webinars, and pep talks with friends weren't going to take the initial step for me, I decided to find that first step on my own. I clicked on a blog that detailed, step-by-step, how to go about creating your own blog. It felt like a starting point. That's about all it felt like, honestly. I had no clue what to do once I created a blog. What would I call it? What would I write about?

I read through the blog and followed the steps as I came across them. I created an account in WordPress and fumbled through the screens and steps until I had a domain name and apparently a host for my site. I didn't even understand what a host was, nor do I really know now, if we're being honest, but I followed the instructions anyway.

WordPress was a step. The domain name was a step. The host for the website was a step. Choosing a design theme to give the website some personality was a step. The colors were a step. Do you see what's happening here? I only set out to do *one* step, but as I took that step, I would come across something that would direct me to what was needed next. Before I knew it, I was half a dozen steps in and the owner of a website. No one knew about the website yet, and I hadn't written an actual blog, but I was further down the road than I had been an hour before.

Without any tech background, I had figured out how get this far. I was officially a blogger, minus writing the first blog, of course. I felt as though I belonged in a quaint coffee shop in Portland. Isn't that where all bloggers write from? As I sat on the couch in my living room that night with my laptop propped up on my thighs, I typed questions into the internet search bar or scanned for a video on YouTube. I kept searching until I came across something that answered my question or showed me how to do something. Much of the time, I couldn't decipher what I was reading, but I continued searching until I could inch another full step out. They were baby steps, but they began to create a path.

What idea has been sitting on your heart and filtering through your mind?

What would be the very first step toward exploring it?

Timing Is Everything—or Is It?

Time. Ah, yes. The only moment that I feel like I have too much time is when I'm running on a treadmill. The clocks on those machines are slower, I just know it.

We can't talk about pursuing purpose and not address the immediate reaction that most people have. "I just don't have enough time." We fool ourselves into thinking we need a vast amount of time to take on any sort of project, but if that were the case, most things wouldn't ever come to fruition. Much like the baby steps we talked about taking earlier, a small amount of time a few times a week to work toward a passion, or on your business, will still get you where you need to be.

Time will be filled whether you intentionally choose to fill it, or not. We don't fill our time as intentionally as we might like to think that we do. We adhere to the clock and make whatever task it is that we're working on fill the time that we have for it. We have all, at some point, worked for an employer and had a set schedule that told us what time to clock in, when to take a lunch, and what time to clock out.

While many of us know what it's like to stay long after the clock-out time has come and gone, we also know that there are days when you have thirty-four minutes before you can clock out, and you're completely caught up. You begin scrolling through Target's website, or maybe you're a better employee than I was and you start reorganizing your email inbox and decluttering your desk drawers. Now, I realize that if your work is done and you walk out the door thirty-four minutes early that your boss might raise an eyebrow. They might dock your pay accordingly. I totally get it. What I want you to realize is that you found a way to fill the time.

Conversely, here's what I also already know about you. I know that if you were given a tight timeline to do something—let's say you have one hour as opposed to normally having two hours—that you would get it done. It's the opposite of filling the time, yes, but you adapt, don't you? You avoid the nonsense that drains your time like checking your text messages, second-guessing which option to choose, getting up to go to the bathroom, or responding to the emails popping up in the lower right hand of your computer screen.

Time, my friend, isn't really the issue. It's whether you let the clock run you, or you run the clock.

Chasing Dreams Before Dawn

I learned quickly that getting up an hour earlier during the week would only be worth it if I could actually get things done. My morning routine is how I transitioned out of my former business. I had to replace myself within the business, balancing two careers for about a year, hiring and training new employees while building a blog, a platform, and an actual business in my spare time. I found five hours a week to work on the new business.

You can find five hours. What you do with that time is entirely up to you. Frankly, it took enough effort to drag myself out of bed at 5:00 a.m. It took equally as much effort to do so without waking up my husband, or worse, waking up one of the kids. If they woke up, the game was over. My kids didn't care whether they woke up at 4:00 a.m. or 9:00 a.m. They immediately wanted to eat breakfast, seek entertainment from Mom, and make noise. My success was reliant upon them remaining asleep, or so I thought.

Though what I do within that hour changes as things progress with my business, the practice of getting up early does not. You may get up some mornings, drink a warm cup of coffee and lose yourself in a book, but I promise you it's a step in the right direction. There will be other mornings that you have that uninterrupted time to put together your social media content for your business page for the entire week in one sitting, or spend most of the hour navigating an online course that is teaching you something that has had you stuck, until now.

I would challenge that the person who says they cannot find the time is the person who doesn't want it bad enough. When you identify that purpose or goal and decide to go for it, you start to take inventory on things in your life—where your time is spent, where your money goes, where your priorities lie—and you begin to make small changes along the way. If you refuse to make even the smallest of changes, then you don't want it bad enough.

I once sat with a financial advisor who had asked me to coffee after we'd met at a networking event. She said, without hesitation, that she could find $200 a month in anyone's budget. She'd never come across a client in fifteen years where she couldn't free up that amount of money at a minimum. She told me this with a sly smile on her face because clients were often adamant that their budgets were in the negative and that they couldn't save a dime. She loved the challenge, I could tell.

She explained that her clients were often strapped paycheck to paycheck until they aligned their priorities with their future. Time works the same way. You have to budget your time. And, friend, I'll tell you the same thing that advisor told me. It's there. There is available time that you're allocating to the wrong things right now.

Since the day I pulled over in front of that house and was brought to tears, I began putting one foot in front of the other. I found the time. When it felt as if there was no time at all, I made it a point to always have my laptop, a book, and my journal with me everywhere I went. When you have a pen/paper or a book or Audible, it's amazing when you'll find spare minutes—waiting in the doctor's office, sitting on the sideline of the soccer field at your kid's practice, or in between appointments. Those fifteen minutes or an hour here and there add up.

If you have what you need to brainstorm, to write, to create material, to make a sales call, or to send an email to someone you met at a networking event, you can use those spare minutes to take an additional step each and every time. My speeches, workshops, my book—much of it has been written during a flight, edited on a soccer field, rehearsed out loud in my car at school pick-up, or brainstormed in spare time in between appointments.

If I waited for an empty day in my calendar or several hours at a time, I wouldn't be as far along as choosing to act within the spare scraps of time pieced together.

What Are You Really Telling Them?

Though a career change felt self-serving, I knew that I was doing this as much for me as I was for my two little girls. My girls watched their mom find her way out of one business and into the launch of another. They don't yet know how hard it's been. They don't know the time, the stress, the money, or the mistakes. They don't know the feeling of defeat or of questioning myself along the way. What they do understand is that mom made up her mind and created a way.

Imagine watching yourself, day in and day out, through the eyes of your child. Do they see you going through the motions, almost stuck in time? Will you be the person who hasn't grown—personally, spiritually, economically—from the time you brought your first child home until the day you drop your youngest off at their college dorm room? Raising children isn't an easy feat, but it's an easy excuse to put yourself last. Will you be the parent who continues to grow as you raise your children? If you feel uneasy answering these questions, that's a good thing. These questions are meant to make you think, they are meant to make you uncomfortable.

Our children learn more by what they see than what we tell them. Little girls grab their mama's heels and pose in front of the mirror not because she told them to, but because they saw the smile and confidence their mom stood with when she was in those heels. They want to feel the way she looked in that moment. Kids learn to hold the door for the person walking in behind them not because they were told to do so, but because their mom or dad does so every time they go somewhere. They are watching, observing, and learning based on what they see, not by what you tell them.

Have you ever watched your child interact with another person? Do you see your demeanor, your facial expressions, or hear the inflection in their voice and it catches you off guard?

Whoa, that was me. I make that face. I use that expression. I stand like that. Yikes, that little facial expression was anything but flattering. I don't want to admit out loud she got that sass from me, but let's be honest, that's coming from me!

Witnessing your child act exactly like you—or your spouse—can be endearing, but it can also be a wake-up call. We aren't as crazy about ourselves when we have a front-row seat to watch ourselves within the little mini-me. Remind yourself, though, that they are also seeing the very best in you.

Chapter Takeaway

A morning routine is about more than enjoying a quiet cup of coffee by yourself. Coffee is just an added bonus. A morning routine is a habit that will keep you focused and intentional on what you prioritize in your life. Routines and habits are consistent, and consistency is ultimately what builds the perseverance you will need when life gets sideways. If life isn't sideways right now, it will be someday. When you face adversity, whether it's in a relationship, your business, an economic downturn, or a need in the family that completely throws your schedule off track, a routine is what will allow you to maintain momentum when others around you are treading water.

Adversity causes us to feel a lack of control. Habits are one aspect of your life that can help you feel a sense of control and calm your nerves in times of uncertainty. They allow you to remain focused when life around you becomes chaotic. The key to any habit is ensuring it works for you. Just because I prefer a wake-up call at 5:00 a.m. doesn't mean that it will work for you.

Even moving the clock thirty minutes earlier can make all the difference in how you approach your day. What time can you commit to waking up and carving out for a morning routine each day? _____

Components of a Morning Routine:

Affirmations:

Draft your own affirmations that you need to incorporate. Use these for goal setting, for self-esteem, or to push through a mental barrier.

1. _____

2. _____

3. _____

Stephanie Hendrick

Gratitude:

Today, I am grateful for _____.

Personal Development:

I commit to _____ minutes per morning to listen to this podcast/
read this book: _____

Prayer/Meditation/Lost in Thought:

Whether you prefer a guided meditation through an app on your phone
or losing yourself in thought, set the amount of time that you can commit
to carving out for yourself: _____

Exercise:

Your schedule may not allow you to work out in the morning. You may
work out in the evenings or on lunch breaks. If it isn't currently part of
your daily routine whatsoever, add thirty minutes to your morning routine
and incorporate some sort of physical activity.

_____ workouts per week / _____ minutes per workout / _____
is where/how I will exercise

3

Step Aside, Sis

I was sitting on our cream-colored, thick carpet in our living room holding Dakota upright, about ten months old at the time, as she tightly grasped a couple of my fingers with her hands for balance. Her face beamed with excitement as she took in her surroundings at this newfound elevation. I watched as her eyes looked all around her, and she squealed with excitement. The world was an entirely new place when you're suddenly a foot higher.

Our dogs could walk right up and lick her in the face, which made her giggle and made me wonder if we'd be visiting the doctor the next day. Her little legs wobbled as she tried to lock her knees and balance. With my arms extended outward for her to balance with, I encouraged her, "Walk toward Mommy. Take a step!" and she'd squeal, take a step toward me, wobble in the knees, and grasp my fingers even tighter as she regained her balance. Then, she'd celebrate with another shriek of delight. It is one of the most tear-filled, joyful moments when you watch your child learning to do something.

Brandon and I had started this evening routine a week or so before, and mostly because our little crawler would quickly scurry down the hall toward the living room when we took her out of her high chair after dinner. We would follow her into the living room, grab a throw pillow off the couch, and prop our backs up against the couch as we sat on the floor, ready to see what she'd try to do.

From an earlier age than you might think, babies start to pick up on the type of emotion that a parent naturally gives them. For us, that meant that when she wanted to play and giggle, she chose Dad. They would play peek-a-boo and silly games he would create on the spot. To this day, a decade later, every single evening (without fail), my husband walks through the door and he's greeted with ear-piercing screeches as our girls sprint down the stairs or the hallway and leap into the air toward him, knowing he'll catch them and swing them around.

As a mom, it's heartwarming to watch this dynamic unfold, though I'd be lying if I said that I often wish I was celebrated every time I walked through the door! As a mom, with my experience anyhow, our girls sought me out when they needed something: a meal, to take them outside to play, to hold when they get hurt, to read them a story, or to take them somewhere. In the most simplified version I can put it: Mom is there for survival, and Dad is there for fun.

That evening, Dakota wanted to show off her balancing abilities for Dad once again. She crawled over to me, grabbed my fingers with each of her warm little hands, and pulled herself up. She took a step toward me, and then another. She glanced back to see Brandon's ear-to-ear smile and encouragement. When she got the reaction she was hoping for, she bent her knees and released my fingers as she softly fell to her bottom, turned over, and crawled over to Brandon to celebrate before she'd continue on to round two.

This time Brandon propped her up, holding her by the waist as she faced toward me, still several feet away. I began to scoot forward toward her.

"No, Steph," he began, "stay further back. She can't take any more steps if you're right in front of her."

I stopped and began to inch my way backward reluctantly. "She hasn't taken more than two steps, and that's with me balancing her."

"I know, but she won't learn if we stay in the way."

He gently released his hands from her waist, and her eyes widened at the realization that she was standing on her own. She threw her arms upward to save her balance as she took a step and then fell backward to her bottom. Shocked for a moment, she realized she was still intact and rolled to her right as she reached for the coffee table to pull herself back up. She faced the table and moved along its side, as she had done several times before, and when she got to the edge, she looked up at me as she turned her body and balanced with her right hand on the table. She took two steps away from the table, squealing as her momentum carried her forward another couple of steps toward me before falling to the soft carpet.

She was walking several steps at a time within a couple days thereafter, and while she would have figured it out at some point along the way, it merely took us getting out of the way in order to allow her to see what she was capable of. Without allowing her to fall, she couldn't learn how to balance. Without coaxing her to try it on her own and watching her fall those first few times, she wouldn't see that it was okay to fall, or that the appropriate response to falling down is merely to get back up rather than to cry and give up.

They Mean Well, I'm Sure

For many of us, our parents tried to control the outcome of certain experiences during our childhood. Their hearts were in the right place as they tried to protect us from tears and from experiencing failure. They knew the feelings of disappointment or heartache and wanted to absorb the pain to prevent us from feeling the full effect. Parents unintentionally hinder their child's coping mechanisms and resilience by removing their ability to ever actually process a tough situation. It's instinctual to preserve, to protect, and to avoid harm. The more we are protected by our parents, though, the less risk we are apt to take as adults. We become comfortable with making decisions that give us a predictable outcome.

Think of the risks you have avoided. Think of the job you took right out of college because you were too scared to start your own business. Think of the relationship you stayed in for too long because you didn't want to face heartache. Think of when you kept quiet in a room full of people because you were afraid of what their opinions would be. Think of the nine-to-five job you're still in because you just aren't quite sure if your little passion project will succeed. Think of the mission trip you won't sign up for because traveling to a third-world country seems dangerous. Think of the inner voice that you continue to ignore because it's nudging you in a direction that doesn't have a clear, guaranteed path.

Stephanie Hendrick

Leaning on Faith Alone

The earliest risk I can remember taking with my husband was when I left my salaried job after having our first daughter. It was a decision that couldn't be resolved by pulling out a piece of paper and writing a new budget in order to say yes or no to this idea. We both agreed that my being home with her was our best option, but this was 2009. We were in the middle of what would later become known as the Great Recession. Brandon's career was in the mortgage industry, which had taken a devastating hit as the housing crisis ensued across the entire country. His income had dropped by fifty percent in 2008, and here we were the following year weighing the stress of dropping to one income.

Noteworthy to mention, this was an income that was entirely commission-based as well. There was no guaranteed salary, and back at that time, most mortgage companies didn't offer health insurance benefits. We would have to incur the cost of private health insurance, as well.

We took the leap of faith, and I quit my job. In hindsight, that decision put us on a trajectory that neither of us could have imagined. Over the next decade, I would work part-time from home to build Brandon's business (which then became *our* business) while the kids napped or were at preschool a couple days per week. The business began to grow and while there were substantial growing pains along the way, that experience is the very reason I can write the chapters in this book today. It's the reason I am hired to coach entrepreneurs, especially those that are (or want to become mothers), on how to most effectively scale and run a business, while raising a family.

The risk of leaving a safe, guaranteed paycheck for a fluctuating single-income household during the greatest recession of our lifetime turned out to be the very journey that God likely had wanted us to take. That risk grew our faith immensely as we saw month after month that He would provide the business that we needed in order to pay our bills and put food on the table. That same risk also put me into a whirlwind of balancing motherhood and a career, but that forced me to find efficiencies and creativity that didn't exist in the industry.

I tapped into a potential that most of us don't realize is within us until we're forced into the position. I believe, to my core, that I had to go on a decade-long journey in order to craft the skills I'd need, garner the resilience and experience, and have the willingness to lean in for the next path He would have waiting for me.

I am not suggesting that you make a drastic change to your life right this moment. What I am suggesting however is that there is a plan for you, and that until you move out of the way, it cannot be revealed or pursued. The easiest decision is always the path of least resistance, but will that help you become who you're meant to be?

I'm a person who likes to visualize things. That is, unless it's visualizing the design of a room (I strive to have a home that Joanna Gaines would walk into and smile with satisfaction as she looked around, but it's not happening for me.) I like to visualize concepts and quotes and stories so that I can understand the wisdom behind them more fully. The idea of us having a purpose for our lives is something that many people struggle with conceptually. It sounds a little woo-woo for them, something only a dreamer might talk about.

Given that purpose for me is a very spiritual thing, there is this visual in my mind that I reflect on in moments where I find myself questioning and doubting what it is I'm truly meant to be doing. It's faith-based, but not written in the Bible. I share it with you in hopes that it gives you the perspective that you need. In moments where my stomach is churning with anxiety and the fear of failure is staring me straight in the face, I like to close my eyes and drop in on a scene (think Ebenezer Scrooge-style—no one knows he's there, and he's just watching things unfold in front of him).

I'm standing off to the side with my arms folded, my right leg crossed in front of my left as I stand on my tiptoes, gently leaning forward with my head turned ever so slightly to the right to hear the conversation taking place a few feet in front of me. There's this little girl, maybe seven years old, with wavy, chocolate-brown hair just past her shoulders and dozens of tiny freckles spread across her cheekbones and nose. She's sitting on an old, wooden chair, her little legs crossed at the ankle and swinging back and forth under the seat. Her hands are tightly together in her lap, and she's looking to her right, where she's having a conversation with a man standing a few feet from her. He has a deep voice with a subtlety of softness as he talks to the little girl. There's a bright beam of sunshine shining through a window behind them. The light is pouring in at an angle, covering the side of his face with a piercing white light. I cannot make out any facial features or skin tones, but I am completely captivated by the scene playing out before me.

The man is telling her that she's been given certain gifts, gifts that are different than the ones that some others have received. He explains that there will be other children and adults with similar passions and gifts, but the combination that each person has been given, coupled with the experiences that await them, is how they each have the ability to serve others and make an impact in this world. His voice quiets to a whisper as he tells her what her purpose is before she leaves the room. The little girl, her nosed scrunched up and eyebrows furrowed as she thinks for a moment, turns and asks the man, "Am I going to forget this when I leave here?"

He nods.

"How will I know I'm serving my purpose if I've forgotten it?"

The man chuckles and reaches for her little hands. As she walks away, she reflects on their conversation, replaying it in her mind. *Follow the passions on my heart and the abilities that come easy. He's created me with certain abilities so that I can seek and live out my purpose— the mission He is giving me. When I feel confused, just pray. He'll always guide me in the direction I need to go.*

This parable that my mind has conjured up ends with just that brief interaction of this little girl talking with God. She'll soon enter the world and begin to be molded by the circumstances and people around her. As she grows, her passions will develop, her abilities will become known and sharpened, and her mind will navigate her through all that she encounters. She'll be met with disappointment, confusion, and heartache at times, though little will she know these are all continuing to shape her into the woman she was once told that she'd need to become.

She'll continue trying, time and time again, despite any failures, in order to someday return to the man and ask, "How did I do?"

Fear, Obligation, and Guilt

I sat on the stiff, gray couch in my business coach's office one Wednesday afternoon. His office sat in the corner of a single-level building with windows stretching floor to ceiling on two of the walls. Through the windows was the backside of the parking lot, which was often empty, and the open desert sat beyond that. On another wall, there was a long whiteboard with notes scribbled in bright blue from a prior client session he'd had. In the center of the room, there was a small, gray couch where I often sat like this particular afternoon, and two upholstered gray chairs, all positioned to face one another.

Brandon and I had hired Jon to coach us into the next phase of our business. We had begun to build our business nearly a decade prior to this point and had grown year after year. We understood, conceptually, how to continue to grow our business, but neither of could quite grasp how we would maintain our current income and work less hours. Working less hours. That was the new goal. Cue hiring a business coach.

In the early months of coaching, Brandon joined me. If you have a partner in your business, it's crucial that you're coached at the same time. Whether you're in a mentorship, a coaching program, or a mastermind, the growth occurs in your mindset. There is a boldness within you that puts blinders on the distractions and fears, opens your eyes to far more possibilities, and a shift in your perception of what is possible. If you go through that without your business partner, you're going to create strife and hinder the progress you're aiming to make.

By coaching together, we were able to create our business plan together and work through the fears we had. Actually, let me clarify. Brandon was able to help *me* work through *my* fears at that point. He's a risk taker, so hiring additional team members and increasing our liability by hundreds of thousands of dollars per year came much easier to him than it was for me. Once we narrowed in on the generalized plan, Brandon backed out of coaching. His strength had always been sales, and from the beginning, we had agreed that I would focus on growth strategy and the operational side of things. Though he loved coaching, we agreed that what was coming next for us—interviewing, hiring, and training new team members, for example—fell in my lane.

Every session with Jon started with a focus on the positive progress that my husband and I had made within the growth of our sales team from the prior two weeks since we'd last met. This week was no different.

"Give me your wins," he said as he walked in holding his black motorcycle helmet in his left hand and his backpack slung over his right shoulder. As he settled into the chair across from me, I started to list out our current sales for the month, the events I had underway to stay in front of referral partners, and how our growing team was doing with training and working together. We celebrated the sales volume and the newest hires we had added to our team.

"This all sounds amazing. What else is going on?" he asked.

I sighed. "Well, I knew this would get harder before it would get easier," I said, "but sometimes, I wonder how I'm ever supposed to back out of this. The new girls are getting along great. It's been a few months now, and they're learning fast. We're super happy with them, but why am I still doing just as much work? I mean, if they're here to replace certain positions that I previously filled, then why am I still having to be this involved? It's been months."

Without a word, Jon stood up and walked over to the whiteboard. He began erasing the blue scribbles from the prior session as he began to unpack what he suspected was going on. "You don't need to be as involved as you are. Not at this point. You're putting yourself in there when you don't need to be. Every single thing you're doing is tied back to fear, obligation, or guilt."

I didn't have an immediate response. I sat in thought, mulling over what he was telling me about myself as he wrote *fear*, *obligation*, and *guilt* up on the board. "Give me some things you're overwhelmed with, or what your day is spent doing. Let's test this out."

We spent the next several minutes hashing out everything from volunteering once a week in Dakota's classroom to showing up in the office every day to being copied on every single email. One by one, Jon began to point out that nothing I was doing was tied back to something I wanted or needed to do. Showing up in the office every single day was a perceived *obligation*. I felt that as a manager it was my responsibility to be physically present every day with the rest of the team, but the reality is that I could do my job from home. Signing up to volunteer every single week in Dakota's classroom was tied to *guilt*. The amount of time I spent working made me feel like a mother choosing work over her child, hence me beginning to overcompensate with volunteering out of guilt. The amount of time I was spending reviewing and double-checking the work of our team members was tied to *fear*. I feared that mistakes would cripple our business. Each of those tasks in small doses—doses in which I freely choose the frequency—would be fine. The problem, as Jon made clear to me that afternoon, was that my day-to-day was being run entirely by emotions that I was not in control of.

Immediately following that session, I began asking myself at each conscious decision if fear, obligation, or guilt were at the core. The next morning, I walked into my home office and sat down. I dialed the newest hire to our team (she had been with us for a good six months by this point) and told her that it was time for her to take the reins on her position. I affirmed her hard work, her attention to detail, and her ability to do the job she was hired to do. She was, as we told every member of our team, the CEO of her own position. It was up to her how she structured her day, how she communicated with clients, and how she handled unexpected issues that were guaranteed to arise. I released control and handed the responsibility to her.

Though it made me nervous, the truth is that every mistake can be figured out. If she made a mistake or upset a client, we could find a solution. We could fix the mistake. We could learn from the mistake. The conversation not only left her empowered to rise to the task at hand but proved in the coming weeks that my inability to step back and let her do things on her own previously was motivated solely by fear. Releasing fear over the what-ifs allowed me to more easily recognize that I also didn't need to be physically present in the office every day. That released obligation from being in control. It also allowed me to drop down to volunteering in my daughter's classroom once or twice a month. I wanted to be there, but I had to realize that I didn't need to be there. That shift released guilt from being in control.

Happiness, purpose, fulfillment, momentum—all of those things are achievable when you release control over the things you ultimately cannot control. Let it go. Stop worrying about every *what if*. Stop creating a contingency plan for every decision you make. Stop allowing perceived obligations to control your schedule. Stop allowing others to make decisions for you. If you're not building your dreams, you're building someone else's.

Chapter Takeaway

Your growth, both personally and professionally, is going to be inhibited more by you than by anyone else. Your desire to control the outcome as often as possible is more about feeling a lack of control subconsciously. The urge for control is fueled by fear and intensified by failure. As you relinquish control, obligation and guilt trick you into thinking you're making the wrong decision. Growth will require you to be aware of what your decisions are fueled by and to question whether or not the decision works for or against you. Releasing the grip that fear, obligation, and guilt have on you is often tied directly to your schedule.

When you plan for the week ahead, you become aware of what you're putting into your schedule. If your schedule feels overwhelming, you'll begin to recognizes the yes that should have been a no.

Pull out your planner (calendar in phone or written planner) and evaluate with these questions:

1. Does your planner give you anxiety? Are you overscheduled?
2. For the appointments giving you anxiety- are they tied to fear, obligation or guilt?
3. Does your schedule allow for you to focus at least one hour per day on the things that will move your passion project or business forward? (Hint: If not, you're very likely overcommitting on those appointments. Removing the unnecessary tasks or appointments is how you will find the scraps of time you need in order to grow in the direction you desire.

4

The Journey Uphill

As I write this chapter at 5:32 a.m. on a Friday morning, McKenna is snuggled under a blanket lying beside me on the couch. While I don't head upstairs to check on the girls until shortly after six o'clock each morning, today was a little different. Like any other morning, I had quietly made my cup of coffee and taken it to my office down the hallway. As I opened my laptop, I could hear the faint background noise of little footsteps on the carpeted stairs just outside my office entryway. I already knew it was McKenna. There was no need to second guess it. Our oldest has acquired the heavy-sleeping talent that only a teenager seems to possess despite being a few years away from that point. It's quite possibly the only teenage trait I am willing to accept at this point. That left our youngest as the only reasonable human being to be awake in the house at that hour.

McKenna walked around the corner, clutching an ivory throw blanket close to her chest, hair disheveled, and eyes squinting at the brightness of my laptop screen. "Hi, Mommy," she began in a tired voice as I reached over and pulled her in for a tight squeeze. "Can you type your book next to me on the couch?"

Now, it isn't common for her to wake up this early these days, but when she does, she loves to simply sit next to me. I grabbed the laptop and followed her down the hallway to the living room, where she snuggled into the soft blanket she'd been carrying and curled up in a tight little ball. I sat beside her and continued to type.

Five minutes later, if even, I heard that same little voice with a hint of sternness. "You type too loud." I smirked as I continued to write, a little more conscious of the *oomph* I was putting into each keystroke thereafter. My efforts went unnoticed and the Sour Patch Kid kicked me back out of the room moments later. I took her request in stride, knowing that it wasn't a complete defeat if she was letting me escape back to my loud typing in another room.

Did I just end up lucky with a child that accepts Mom is up early to work on herself and her projects at the crack of dawn? No. Don't worry. This was not—and sometimes still is not—my normal. There have been mornings when this same squeezable, loveable, cute little munchkin comes into the room and insists that we watch *Boss Baby* together, pull out a board game, or make a craft that inevitably involves paints or glue guns. On those mornings, I have to choose my battle. Do I put my foot down and have her wake up the rest of the household when she's faced with an answer she doesn't like? Hypothetically, yes, that's what we should do as parents. I know that's what you're expecting me to say, so let's just put that option on the table. I'm on board with it, in theory. But not at 5:00 a.m. Let's be honest—if she wakes up the rest of the household, I'm then dealing with three cranky children. Five o'clock in the morning has an entirely different set of rules for this short season of our lives, as far as I'm concerned.

Not every morning, day, or week is going to go as expected. You can do all the planning and backup planning, but inevitably you will have moments that go awry. Your daughter will wake up with a fever in the middle of the night. Your son will ask you no less than fifty-two questions about his homework while you're trying to finish those last few tasks for the day. The meeting you are pee-your-pants excited about will be rescheduled. The first eighty-seven pitches you send to podcast hosts won't even receive an email reply. The manufacturer creating your product will have delays.

Okay, truth be told, I am not trying to be Debbie Downer. Actually, quite the contrary. I want to acknowledge that the I-can't-believe-this-is-happening-right-now moments happen to all of us. Don't allow them to completely derail you from what you're working on. When you learn to adapt to the unexpected, you're more apt to take a deep breath, make yourself present in the moment, and pick up where you left off when that moment has passed.

Not Quite Your Sorority Girl

When I was a sophomore in college, I had a full-time job and lived in an apartment off-campus. I would love to tell you about the sorority I joined, the spring breaks in Cancun, and all the home football games in the huge stadium, but none of it would be true. Luckily for me, smartphones weren't out in 2005, so I wasn't even aware of what I was missing. Facebook was brand new and hadn't spread across the college campuses yet.

My parents had just divorced, my mom was struggling financially just to keep a roof over hers and my brother and sister's heads, and my dad had moved back East to try and get back on his feet, sober up, and find a job. I was adamant that my circumstances would not keep me from pursuing college, but *college life* wasn't an option on the table.

Working full-time while going to school full-time was a balancing act. Freshman year, I worked as a bank teller at a local credit union. The manager had a staff of mostly college kids, so we would submit our class schedules, and she would build our part-time work schedules around that. When I moved out onto my own the summer before sophomore year, I was slapped in the face with more responsibilities. I knew I would have to pay rent, electricity, and buy my own groceries, but what I didn't realize was how my entire life would have to be shaped around that responsibility. The full-time job was now a necessity, not a decision. I took a position at a mortgage company hoping I could clock-in and clock-out effortlessly and focus on my studies the next few years.

I found myself working 8:30 a.m. to 5:00 p.m., racing over to campus for classes, and leaving at 9:30 at night a few nights a week. The only issue that had initially come up (outside of the days being so long) was that I couldn't find the math class—a required class for my degree—in the evening. After pushing it off for a semester, the same issue popped up the following semester. No evening classes. I was going to fall behind if I couldn't take that class, given it was a prerequisite for other classes I would still have to take.

I couldn't take a midday class because my employer wouldn't allow it. Should I quit my job? Could I find another job with similar pay in order to focus on my classes? Should I just change my major to something that didn't require math? The obvious answer wasn't jumping out at me, but it didn't change the fact that a decision had to be made.

No Obvious Choices

What do you do when you feel backed into a corner? Do you ever find yourself continuously reviewing—and rereviewing—the options just in case you suddenly realize something you hadn't before? That's about as useful as when you're bored and you walk over to the pantry and open the doors. You stare awhile, close the doors, and walk away when nothing looks satisfying. Five or ten minutes go by, and, without realizing it necessarily, you're back at the pantry again staring at the food choices on the shelves in front of you. Still nothing appetizing. *Okay, maybe in a few more minutes. Maybe I'll check again then and change my mind about the menu options.*

So often, we find ourselves at a crossroads where neither option is appealing. Both options would require us to rearrange our lives a bit. This is where most people get stuck. They won't tell you that they've given up, just that the timing hasn't worked out so far, or that there aren't any realistic options. They convince themselves that there are no options remaining and that they've gotten as far as they can.

One of my favorite books, *The Seven Decisions* by Andy Andrews, talks about the persistent decision. Andy explains this promise we have to make to ourselves if we are to accept this particular decision.

> I will persist without exception. To achieve the results I desire, it is not even necessary that I enjoy the process. It is only important that I continue the process with my eyes on the outcome.

Sometimes, all the options on the table are less than ideal. They just are. Despite our reluctance to accept that life isn't unfolding exactly as we had it pictured in our minds, know that the tough moments reshape the mold of who you are. What you endure today shapes who you become tomorrow.

Uncomfortable Became Comfortable

As a college student needing to pay my rent and also pass my classes to maintain an academic scholarship, I often felt backed into a corner when my work and school schedules conflicted. School represented my future, but work provided for my present well-being. Initially, the only options in front of me were to fall behind in my coursework and graduate later than planned or find a new job with flexible hours and similar pay. A third option dawned on me one day. I reached out to my counselor and asked if I could find a comparable course at a community college and have it transferred over for credit. Given that it was a prerequisite course, that option was acceptable. All I had to do was find a community college that offered the course I needed. I reviewed class schedules for a handful of community colleges (there are several in the Phoenix area) and found one available class. One campus. One course offering. It was at 7:00 a.m., twice per week. It was also about an hour drive from where I lived. *Deep sigh.* But it was an option.

This wasn't the easy option. There's nothing easy about taking classes before and after a full day of work, getting home around 10:00 p.m. at night, and pulling back out of the driveway by 6:00 a.m. the next morning. It was uncomfortable. It was mentally draining. I was tired. I was burning out. But I also knew it was temporary. I knew that it would get me closer to my goal. The days were incredibly long, but I began to understand that there is always a choice. The choice may not be ideal, but the choice is always there. The early-morning hours, when I could have slept in a little bit longer, are ultimately what propelled me to the next step in the road ahead.

Years later—a decade later, actually—when I finally had a grasp on what I should be doing with my life (because it doesn't come naturally to all of us by high school graduation), I was faced with two less-than-desirable options once again. As you already know by now, I had decided to leave the business that my husband and I had grown together. At that point, our business could not run without me in some capacity every single day. Imagine yourself (or maybe you don't have to, maybe this is you right now) in everyday life with your work, with projects, with your own business, perhaps. You have momentum, things are progressing, and the income is where you've always desired it to be. The only issue is *inside* of you, inside your head and your heart. You're doing something you haven't really envisioned for yourself, something that you're good at but not passionate about. You're a keystone in someone else's dream.

To walk away at this level of success seems ludicrous. *Now isn't the right time*, you tell yourself. Truth be told, you don't know when, or if, there ever would be a right time. Walking away or replacing yourself would be risky financially, incredibly stressful and time-consuming, and the idea makes your stomach do flip-flops. Have you been there?

That's where I was. Again. Stuck. The two options were to abruptly quit and walk away, leaving my husband to deal with the ramifications (which probably would put quite a strain on our marriage, mind you), or to somehow begin the long, painstaking process of hiring, training, and replacing myself. Ugh. There I was, with two matter-of-fact options again. Neither had an appeal, but seldom is opportunity waiting for you tied with a pretty, pink bow.

Shifting the Clock

Given I still have a marriage very much intact, you might already have guessed I chose the latter option. It's tough to allow a process to take place when everything inside of you is excited, eager, and ready to run full force for what you feel called to pursue next. The eagerness to begin to put together my vision for a speaking and writing career was going to take a lot of time, a lot of trial and error, and vision. Those were all things I couldn't necessarily work on during the day, at least not in large blocks of uninterrupted time.

Working after the kids went to bed at night wasn't sustainable. I wasn't productive in the evening and just wanted to relax after a stressful day. Giving up the short amount of time that I got to spend alone with my husband before I fall asleep was something I didn't want to compromise on. I wasn't willing to part with it, and I'm sure he's grateful for that. That left me in a position to either put my aspirations on hold for several months, until I had hired and trained enough employees to fully transition myself out of the business, or to create more time in the day. I remembered the younger, college-age version of myself that woke before dawn to get across town for that math class. The early mornings that had propelled me forward years earlier were once again the solution I needed for this next chapter in my life.

Initially, I began getting up an hour earlier in the mornings. Was it easy? No. Let me be super honest with you. There were several mornings that I hit snooze and stayed in bed for another hour. There were other mornings I did get up, got to the coffee pot quickly enough, and saw what I could accomplish in a quiet setting before the chaos of kids, emails, and texts would begin coming in. On the days that I allowed myself to sleep through the hour, I would feel guilt during the day. I would feel that I missed out on an opportunity to take another baby step closer to realizing my vision. I began to tap into my mindset and anticipate the inevitable feelings that I knew would come each morning if I didn't show up for myself before dawn. I needed that little voice of motivation in the mornings to get me up and moving. I took a sticky note and a sharpie and wrote down "Hitting snooze pushes your dream off another day."

As odd as it may sound, I needed that coaching, even if the note was from *me*. I needed the reminder that every day got me a little bit further along, but only if I showed up. The only person who knows your excuses is you. The only person who knows what motivates you is you. Anticipate the dialogue in your own head. You already know how it's going to play out, so why not create the workaround so that you can implement your project, your workout, or your business?

If you know that you often miss your workouts in the afternoon because of, well, life, then you can plan for that distraction. You can shift it to the morning before anything or anyone has a chance to call, email, text, or scream at you. You owe it to yourself to take care of the body you were given, take care of your health, and give yourself that time to clear your head and sweat out the stress or anxiety. I understand that you might not be a morning person, but if you aren't accepting any of your other options, then you have a decision to make. Maybe it's time to stop telling yourself who you aren't and redefine who it is you want to *become*.

Stephanie Hendrick

Define the Who, Not the Do

I was listening to a pastor one Sunday morning shortly after the start of the year, and he was talking about New Year's resolutions. He gave a staggering statistic about the success rate of New Year's resolutions. You and I both already know resolutions are seldom kept through the course of the year, but do you know how bad the results are? It was somewhere in the vicinity of only 20 percent of people still working on their resolution by Valentine's Day, and then it dropped to a mere 8 percent of people who would implement the resolution long term. A whopping 92 percent of people just completely give it up, walk away, and resort to what was more comfortable, regardless of the ramifications.

The pastor went on to explain that one of the most detrimental decisions we make is to define *how* or *what* we will do as part of the resolution, as opposed to defining *who* it is that we want to be. It's sounds like such a subtle change, but he had my attention. He went on to explain that by identifying who you are aiming to be, it completely changes the way you approach a decision in your life. Creating action steps are important, but if the person that is walking those steps hasn't changed on the inside, then how can they be expected to continue with the steps that they've suddenly decided to put into place? In theory, what he was saying made sense to me, but only because I knew what to do with it. If you're a skeptic, don't worry.

When I decided to write this book, I knew it would take a huge time commitment. While it might seem like an author can knock out one or two thousand words in a couple hours, it's not as simple as that. There are days when the words just don't appear on paper. There are days when the inspiration isn't there. There are days when I wonder who I am to write this book. It's on all of these types of days that I have to know exactly *who* I am, *who* I am becoming and *who* I am showing up as day after day to keep me from shutting the laptop and walking away from it all. You see, when I decided to write this book, I had to change my inner dialogue, my identity, and how I talked about what I was doing. I became an author overnight. I began to affirm in my journal each morning that I was a best-selling author—all before I had even written the first chapter.

I continued to write that same sentiment every single morning. It was an affirmation, one of a handful that I had written for months on end.

As you write out an affirmation (or recite it in a mirror to yourself), it seeps into your subconscious and transforms you from the inside out. You need to envision who it is you aspire to be, and then you need to begin to recognize yourself as that person. You need to convince yourself of who you are and what you're worthy of before you can convince anyone else.

Affirmations aren't as *woo-woo* as I once thought them to be. I was first introduced to them by my business coach. He explained that our subconscious mind actually drives our conscious decisions. Your subconscious doesn't know what is and isn't real, so when we tell ourselves who we are or what we've accomplished, our subconscious will begin to direct us toward decisions that align with that goal since it believes we've already achieved it. This is more of a brain hack than anything.

I'm not concerned with who you are right now. My goal is to push you toward who you will become. There is untapped potential within you, but before I can give you the tools to implement to pursue your business, project, or vision, I need to help you convince yourself that you are capable of it.

Let's go back to the *woo-woo* affirmations for a minute. When my own business coach pushed me to begin this practice, I had two affirmations that I began with—one that worked on my self-perception and one that pertained to a business goal.

They were,

1. What other people think of me doesn't matter.
2. My team closes five million dollars in sales volume each month. (This had to do with the business my husband and I ran together. In case you're wondering, no, this didn't mean we made five million dollars per month (or year), or even remotely close to that. The math doesn't quite work like that.)

You can tell from the first one that I struggled—a lot—with how I was perceived by others. I was in a season of life for several years (it was a long season) where I didn't feel as though I fit in anywhere. I was co-managing a sales team with my husband in an industry dominated by men. I wasn't recognized equally for my hand in our success. In fact, it was actually my husband (God Bless that man) who finally stood up and began to tell people in our industry what my role truly looked like, what I was responsible for, and what I was capable of.

My struggle for self-worth wasn't just with peers in my industry. I felt isolated from friends and other women my age who hadn't yet had children. My day-to-day was different than theirs. They struggled with where to go to happy hour on Thursdays, and I worried about when to wean my baby off of a pacifier. I was unable to identify with colleagues (men) and unable to fit in with women I had known for years. Without realizing what was happening at the time, I had begun to retreat and become hypersensitive to what others thought of me.

To this day, I still recite that affirmation to myself each morning. It's programmed as a recurring appointment within my phone because while I have made immense progress with my self-worth, I believe people's opinions can create unnecessary noise within us. I keep that one tucked closely to my heart to remind me that my worth isn't determined by others.

Friend, your self-worth isn't determined by others either. You were perfectly and beautifully made, and if you feel less-than in any way, if you struggle with comparison, or if you are in a rut, give that affirmation a try. It will take time. Write it on your mirror, set a timer for it to pop up on your phone, and write it daily. Clutch onto the statement that you are worthy of who you are and who you will become because I can promise you that brighter days are coming for you.

The second affirmation is somewhat of a fun one because it was the first affirmation that ever came true. At the time, our sales volume was averaging $2.5M per month. Yet, daily, I was telling myself that our team was producing double that amount. I was saying it in the present tense when I wrote out the affirmation and in a manner that it was fact—that it had already been accomplished and continued to be so.

Some may think that this was wishful thinking. It wasn't. It was a mindset. It was a way of managing, hiring, training, marketing, and strategizing in a manner consistent with a higher performance than we'd ever known. While describing the decisions and the day-to-day would be several chapters in and of themselves, I can tell you that we made bold moves in the months that followed. We knew that in order to grow we needed more infrastructure, which meant hiring another employee and delegating activities to an outside marketing company before the growth would occur.

This is where many business owners and managers hit the invisible ceiling. They want to expand and burst at the seams before they bring on an additional expense. We went against that limiting approach. We invested in our business, in our future, and in a new person. Less than a year after I had implemented that affirmation into my routine, I can remember looking at a report one morning and realizing it had all come to fruition.

This wasn't a stroke of luck. It wasn't a matter of business growth just catching up with the affirmation. Initially, that's what my husband thought when I ran into the bedroom and told him what I had calculated. I was giddy and had a grin ear to ear. Truth be told, I wasn't celebrating the number. I was celebrating that the affirmation had worked. I didn't truly believe affirmations had an ability to do much at all until that moment. I was celebrating that my mindset had shifted and allowed us to make decisions over the prior few months that could've otherwise kept us on an even keel for sales volume. Only in hindsight could I see the decisions that seemed out of character from the girl I'd been the year before.

Those two affirmations mirrored back to me who I was becoming, who I wanted to be at the time. My affirmations have evolved since then, and they now focus on the purpose I identified for this season of my life- the speaker on stages across the nation sharing her message with women and the author whose book you're now holding in your hands.

My point is this: it goes beyond setting a simple action step. Yes, the action step might show that, for me, I block out a couple hours at a time a few days a week for the brainstorming, the research, the outline, and table of contents to guide me, or the writing itself. But when distractions pop up (and they inevitably will) and the doubts creep in, knowing who it is we are, who we're striving to be, is what will bring you back to the action steps when you would otherwise veer away from the steps altogether.

Chapter Takeaway

Now it's your turn. Let's build out the affirmations that identify who you want to be. If you have specific goals in mind, write out the goal as if you've already accomplished it. For example, let's say you are a Realtor and want to sell five homes per month. You might only be selling one to two per month right now, but this is how you would write it out: "I sell five homes per month."

If you're unsure of where to start, think of a limiting belief you have about yourself. What are you insecure about? For example, you might feel as though the only time you spend with your kids is bathing, cooking, and cleaning up after them. The guilt of not having those special moments to bond with them or have fun begin to wear on you. Cue mom guilt. Your affirmation might look like this: "I am an exceptional and present mom to my children."

Now, it's your turn:

1.

2.

3.

Next, decide when and how you will implement these affirmations. Will you sit down and write them in a notebook? Will you set them on your phone calendar so that they automatically pop up in front of you each day (or multiple times per day)? Will you write them on your bathroom mirror, or on a sticky note on your nightstand? Be intentional.

5

The Thirty-Hour Work Week

When I was in the seventh grade, I begged my parents for a pager. Do you remember those? My mom had a pager for work, and I would watch her clip it to the pocket of her jeans when she was on-call. If you aren't familiar with a pager, think of it as a small, black box about the length and width of a credit card, with a sliver of a screen on one edge of it. It would beep, a phone number would appear, and she'd call the person who was trying to reach her. It was the earliest form of text messaging I guess you could say, except it had no letters or emojis.

If you were trying to send a message, you were better off just picking up the phone. If you're still not quite sure what a pager is, turn on any TV show that takes place in a hospital. Eventually, you'll hear a beep, watch the doctor look down at the device clipped to their scrubs, and see them race to save the day.

In all its glory, that little teal-colored beeping box made its way to me on my thirteenth birthday wrapped in the Sunday comics. (Like any frugal mother, mine found a way to repurpose the daily newspaper.) I ran to the oak colored, L-shaped desk that sat in our living room and grabbed a piece of white paper from the back of our printer and a purple pen. Over the next twenty minutes, I wrote my new pager number and name onto strips of paper to hand out at school the next day.

Now, for context, let me also tell you what other amazing technology existed at this time—to either take you down memory lane or to help paint the picture if all you've ever known are iPods, iPads, and smartphones (only the cell phone existed at this time, and no one owned one). When your bestie would page you, you would run to the home phone and call her back. However, your home phone line was often shared by your home computer for this new-era technology called the internet.

Hold on. Before we go any further, we have to talk about what the internet was for most of us back then. It wasn't a Google page that you opened. In every household I was aware of at the time, it was AOL (America Online). Access to the internet came through a subscription you had to purchase. Luckily, AOL would mail the masses a CD every few months with 100 free hours of internet usage. However, accessing the internet would then mean you were tying up your phone line. If someone was instant messaging (IM'ing, as we referred to it) their friends on AOL, you weren't calling your bestie back after she paged you. Instead, you were waiting.

So, like any wise teenager, you would walk up behind your younger sister and tell her she had exactly five minutes left to finish her IMs, or else you were pulling the phone cord out of the wall. Technology brought out the best in teenage girls.

My parents eventually got a second phone line that my sister and I could share. They began to realize that they had become unreachable by anyone from the outside world as a result of having a teenager and preteen who occupied the phone line in some fashion for, well, the entire evening. Truth be told, this just meant one of us could be on the internet (tied to the home phone line) while the other could chat with her girlfriends on our new second phone line. While that helped settle the nightly battle between my younger sister and me, my parents were still unreachable to the outside world.

Two years later, freshman year of high school, pagers were a thing of the past. I sat at one of my best friend's birthday parties and watched her open her presents. She opened scrunchies, CDs, clothes, and gift cards, until one gift remained. It was from her grandparents. Our little jaws hit the floor when we saw what was in the small rectangular box. It was a cell phone. I'm not even sure if her parents owned cell phones yet. It was the Fall of 2000, and cell phones were just beginning to infiltrate households—teeny tiny little green screens and an antenna that you would pull up before you made a call.

For Millennials, the era of technology was a fast-paced, ever-changing one. Within a span of a couple years, we were introduced to pagers, wireless phones, the internet, voicemail systems being moved from an actual recording box to being something you dialed into from your landline, CDs, and cell phones. Less than a decade later, we'd be introduced to a platform called social media, *widespread* internet, laptops, and smartphones that would give us access to virtually anything at any time simply by reaching into our back pocket.

It's about the Approach, Not the Clock

Though the internet and cell phones changed what our day-to-day lives looked like and shaped younger generations, our culture in many ways has failed to adapt. We see people working eight or more hours a day, despite how much quicker communication is nowadays. A couple decades ago, you would send a fax to transmit a document instead of scanning and emailing it back. Homes and offices often had huge, steel filing cabinets to keep copies of paperwork and receipts. Now, everything is scanned and saved in a cloud somewhere. Many companies hold meetings virtually instead of having an entire room full of people commute into the office and lose two hours of their day on the freeway. Do you see how many things have become faster, easier, and less time-consuming?

What was accomplished in eight hours a couple decades ago you can do in far less time today. The efficiencies have allowed society to produce more, accomplish more, and make more than was ever possible before. This left companies and entrepreneurs with a choice: cut back the hours worked and reap the same result or work the same hours and reap far more.

You already know how this story goes. Companies chose increased profit margins over less time in the office. They chose to keep their workforce in place for the same costs and the same amount of time, but with substantially higher output and profits as a result of all the efficiencies that technology has afforded us.

80/20

In the early 1900s, Vilfredo Pareto created a mathematical equation that helped demonstrate the disparity of wealth in the Italian economy at the time. *Oh, did I forget to mention you're in history class right now? Hang with me. This is actually pretty interesting. Promise.*

Known as Pareto's Principle, and later referred to as the 80/20 Rule, it theorized that eighty percent of the nation's wealth is created by twenty percent of the population. Though Pareto was only trying to apply this principle to the Italian economy with that theory, the 80/20 Rule caught on in the business world because the principle held true when applied to business in general. You've heard one of the following, I'm sure,

80 percent of a business's revenue comes from 20 percent of its customers.

80 percent of a business's sales are generated by 20 percent of the salesforce.

80 percent of donations come from 20 percent of the total donors.

80 percent of your progress comes from 20 percent of your productivity.

That last one, phew. It's kind of depressing, isn't it? Yeah, most of what you're doing isn't actually moving the needle.

Okay, so what am I saying? Drop the rest of what you're doing because it's not as pertinent? No. Not exactly. I'm bringing Pareto's Law to your attention because sometimes your mind needs a little perspective. You need to take a step back in order to evaluate what is working and what isn't, what is productive and what is merely time-consuming, what is giving you momentum and what is only passing the time.

This Isn't Grandma's Generation

I want to have an open conversation with you about how much things have shifted in our culture. If you and I fail to acknowledge what has changed and what has remained the same then we'll never be on the same page. This conversation is not only about the dynamic of the modern household, but about the increased workload placed on women that no one seems to be talking about. Until now.

We don't need data (though a lot of it exists) to agree that women have been shifting more and more into the workforce instead of staying at home to raise tiny humans and run a household. But why? Sure, some women find themselves as single mothers and have to work to support their family. Other women find that a dual-income household is the only viable option in their family. Other women feel an inner desire to pursue something and are chasing the ambition that prior generations of women were told to turn their attention away from.

Grandma didn't have that opportunity, nor was she necessarily looking for one. Grandma and Grandpa probably also didn't have two cars, a couple vacations per year, expensive sports teams for their kids, or college tuition bills to the tune of, well, a fortune. Those aren't necessities, by any means, but let's be honest—in many cases, this modernized lifestyle we're seeing often requires a dual income.

Your grandparents were able to comfortably live off Grandpa's income because times were much simpler. Did they have a house cleaner? Probably not. Did they each have SUVs with hefty payments almost totaling the same as a mortgage payment? Definitely not. Did Grandma have her hair dyed, eyelash extensions filled, nails manicured, and Botox done? I'm willing to bet she didn't. Ridiculous, over-the-top birthday parties for her kids? Amazon Prime deliveries every day? No and no.

The lifestyle that we know today didn't exist for those generations. They were simpler times. Today's less-than-simplistic lifestyle is one huge driver behind this cultural shift of so many women going into the workforce.

But there's another driving force behind the cultural shift that is seeing women seek higher education, create small businesses, and strive to make waves in the corporate world. This is the one I want to focus on. It's *opportunity*. It's being told from a young age that they have the potential to do anything that they desire. It's the permission to listen to that quiet voice in their head and take a step in a different direction.

Now, let me stop you before you head toward a road that I'm not following you down. This isn't about whether women should stay home or not. This conversation is not suggesting that every woman should create a business or nonprofit. This conversation isn't about family dynamic. This conversation most certainly isn't suggesting that your purpose cannot be found as a SAHM. It most certainly can, and I know plenty of women who do feel their purpose is at home raising their littles right now.

I also know plenty of women who stay home with their children and run businesses out of their home. Do you see the *opportunity* I was referring to earlier? The opportunity is the very choice that women have in regards to creating a life they love. Women nowadays can design their lives, decide what they want different seasons of life to look like, and that's what makes life today so vastly different than the generations before us. We have permission to pursue a purpose outside of cooking three meals and vacuuming the living room every day. Do you grasp that? It's a big, big deal.

The purpose we feel called to right now may look different next year or a different season of life. It's all a journey, and each season prepares us for the next. I want to be crystal clear that this conversation isn't divisive. This is simply a conversation about the ability for women pursue careers or passion projects while still carrying substantial responsibilities with kids, commutes to and from school, spouses, laundry, soccer practice, dance class, and wherever else any minivan on the road is headed.

The Micro Shift Right Underneath Our Noses

Around 2010 or so, with smartphones and social media infiltrating society, an opportunity began to present itself. The women who had followed their calling to stay home with those tiny humans began starting businesses out of their homes. Now, this certainly existed prior to 2010, but new technologies since then have completely broadened the opportunity for women to do this. Female entrepreneurs (okay, honestly every entrepreneur has this, but I want to stay on topic here) have the flexibility to create a business and a schedule that can mold over time and that didn't exist before this technology. Many female entrepreneurs seek to run their own businesses long before children because they want the flexibility if and when the day does come that they welcome a little one into the world.

Etsy shops, social media account managers, bloggers, MLMs, nutrition coaches, telehealth—the list goes on. It's a long one, isn't it? The opportunities are endless and women are combining their passions with a new platform that allows them to put mom-wife-business together in a more manageable way. That's a drastic change and a welcomed one, but let's be honest. It causes all sorts of new stresses. Without boundaries, you'll lose yourself in a vortex of mom guilt and a business that will plateau.

As a mom of two ridiculously energetic little girls, I came to realize very quickly that running a household, building a business, and navigating parenthood made my weeks run thin. Super thin. Eight-hour days (which, honestly often became ten-plus-hour days diced between the wee hours of the morning, several hours throughout the day, and then again late at night) often felt as though they were consuming every ounce of the energy I had left over after nursing a baby throughout the night, shuttling kids all over town, and putting a couple of food groups together at the last minute and calling it dinner.

This phenomenon of Super Mom, as we know her, is short-lived. I can promise you, if you haven't experienced it already, that you will sacrifice in one area of your life in order to compensate in another. As embarrassing as it is to admit, I was initially so consumed by my workload and having a newborn all at once that I would respond to emails while I was breastfeeding. The anxiety of how much my inbox would accumulate with tasks and emails in just a half hour overwhelmed me to the point of multitasking. Multitasking everything. Do you multitask well? I bet you *think* you do. But should you? Nope.

Where is it, in your day-to-day, that you feel the most stress? When are you most apt to multitask? Multitasking is what I like to think of as a cold remedy. When you start to feel congested and know that a cold has crept in, you respond by doing what? You might grab a chamomile tea, take some zinc lozenges, or drink lots of fluids to push it through your system. But it's already set in. Sure, the zinc lozenge and fluids might push it through your system quicker than it otherwise would, but the cold or virus is already inside your body.

In the same way that you respond to the cold symptoms, multitasking is how you respond when you already have too much on your plate. A to-do list that reaches the floor is causing you anxiety whether you realize it or not. You're multitasking to curb the side effects of what you've taken on.

Evaluate your day-to-day. You know *when* you tend to multitask and that it's the sign of you already juggling too many things. We're going to begin to shift your perspective on where time should be spent, how much time to spend on things, where to invest money, and when to delegate—all of which are to enable you to design the life you're after in order to pursue your purpose to its fullest potential. In order to do so, you need to openly recognize the stressors in your life and begin to reconcile that change must take place in order to allow for growth.

Freedom Isn't Inside a Cage

My husband told me a story recently about two red-tailed hawks. He began to describe to me that these two predatory birds had been injured and taken in by a wildlife rehabilitation center. The rehabilitation center nursed these wild birds back to health while keeping them in caged areas to prevent them from trying to fly. They knew the birds couldn't return to the wild before they had fully healed.

Weeks went by, and the birds had made a full recovery and were ready to be returned to the wild. One morning, they opened the cages, and the birds flew out and back into the wild just as intended. To everyone's surprise, the hawks returned that night to their cage. The employees of the rehabilitation center weren't sure what to think, so they left the door to the cage open so that the birds could fly back out. When the sun rose, the birds flew out and into the wild, but returned again that night. Day after day, the birds—free of captivity—returned at night to their cages. Over time, however, the birds stopped leaving their cages. The door was still open, yet they remained within the safety of the cage. These wild hawks were completely free to leave at any given time, yet their freedom was lived out in the confines of a cage. A cage that you and I are fully aware of, but that they didn't seem to recognize.

Listening to the story of the hawks, it dawned on me that you and I often live our lives restricted by a cage, one that *we* don't even see, but that we exist within. We have abilities and the freedom to create a life that we love, but we fail to recognize that we're the ones choosing to remain within the confines of the cage. This cage could be an employer that you're afraid to leave because the thought of branching out on your own is terrifying. It feels like an overwhelming risk. The cage could be a relationship with a colleague, peer, family member, or friend who tells you your ideas are a little too ambitious. The cage could be that you're living your life in thirty-minute increments in order to get ninety-two things done today before you have to make dinner. The cage could be your own mind telling you that settling for what has been given to you is better than pursuing what is waiting for you if you would step outside the door.

The red-tailed hawks were capable of living the life intended for them. Instead, they will never reach their full potential. They settled. The same is true for you each time you choose to conform to what society tells you to do rather than following that inner nudge to create your own path. While we can learn from others that chased similar dreams, we have to remain open to the idea that our own minds are capable of guiding us further than we realize.

Caged In by the Clock

When I came to understand this concept, I revisited the idea of the forty-hour workweek. There I was, a sleep-deprived mom to two little girls, a wife trying to figure out how to cook healthy meals, get to the gym to shed pregnancy weight, spend an inkling of time with my husband, and show up as an equal partner in a business that was growing faster than we could keep up at the time. Phew! It was a lot.

I began to take myself through a series of questions that I want to ask you now:

1. **What does your ideal day look like?**
   For starters, let me preface by saying that this ideal day will change over time, especially for parents. When you have babies or toddlers, you might work from home with the kids there. A few years later, the littles are in preschool a couple days per week. When they get to school age, your schedule changes again. Suddenly, that 7:00 a.m. workout you'd been doing doesn't fit anymore because 7:00 a.m. is when you're hunting down the missing homework or trying to find the one and only shirt that your child wants to wear to school that day. Your day will then have an abrupt pause in the midafternoon when you pick them up from school. This can look a thousand different ways, but the point is to focus on what you

want your ideal day to look like *right now* (with the acceptance that this will inevitably change at some point).

2. **Does this ideal day incorporate time for what is important to you?**
    When I work with clients and we unpack their ideal days, they tend to focus solely on their work. While I'm a business coach and can fully understand why they answer me this way, it's really important that you understand that the way you design your life is fully within your control, and therefore, it's really important to set the boundaries, the non-negotiables, and the expectations upfront so that they're incorporated from the beginning. Ask yourself if this ideal day and timeline leaves you time to get your energy levels up and narrow your focus. Ask yourself if you've intentionally carved out time for the type of spouse, parent, business partner, friend, coach or whomever you want to show up as. There was a reason you chose to work at home, start a business, or venture down your current path. Somewhere along the way, things got a little off track, and the benefits began to fade. Let's bring those back into focus. Remind yourself of what's important to incorporate into your day.

3. **What are the time suckers in your life?**
    For a moment, throw every rational thought out of your head. I have to tell you this, or else you won't fully think through this question. Where do you lose time? Where are there spare moments where you sacrifice time? If you're feeling stuck, let me walk you through some possible areas that you might be losing time. Do you commute to appointments with clients, drive across town to an office, or drop kids off at school? Do you always seem to have some sort of appointment—nonwork-related—that you're running off to, such as getting your nails or lashes done, running to dry cleaner, pediatric appointment, or to the dentist? Until you stop and think through how often you are en route to one of these types of obligations, you may not realize how often these are popping

up in your schedule. List them out, and we'll address how to intentionally schedule these in a bit.

4. **What are your typical day-to-day activities in your business?** Every business or project is going to look different. When you're in a productive mode, what are the different facets you have to manage in order to sustain your business? Think about every aspect such as designing products, creating or ordering supplies or products, writing blogs, meeting with team members, creating marketing material, social media branding and posts, phone calls or meetings with clients, accounting, and behind-the-scenes planning for the events, projects, or promotions. You and I both know this list could go on for several pages if we try to encompass every type of business and how they might create, promote, sell, and manage their business. For this exercise, focus on the common day-to-day activities, not the infrequent tasks that come up.

Putting the Pieces Together

After working through these questions, you should have a whiteboard or page filled with ideas, visions, and a timeline. The intent of this exercise isn't to scale back your business but instead to look at scaling back the *time* that it consumes. While that will sound counterintuitive to most people, I can attest firsthand that this is 100 percent possible. This is how I took a forty-hour workweek and scaled it back to thirty hours.

Let's revisit the questions, and I'll walk you through my own answers. While my answers likely won't match yours (and that's okay, they shouldn't), it will show you possible areas to consider that you might not have before and that it's absolutely possible to increase your productivity by reworking your calendar and priorities.

What does my ideal day look like? Remember: this schedule will change over time and started much differently than how my day looks today. It also flows much differently if I'm traveling for work versus working at home. Working through this exercise, I focused on a typical day from my home office.

5:00–6:00 a.m.: Morning routine (We touched on this in chapter 4.)—What I utilize this time for changes with time, but it's always with intention. I avoid emails, social media, text messages, and conversations with any humans in my household. The dogs are fair game. The focus here is on personal development (reading), gratitude (journaling), and affirming my goals (more journaling), and a portion of time to work on any given project for my business.

6:00–7:15 a.m.: The dogs and I head upstairs to wake up the girls, snuggle in their beds with them for a few minutes and then make lunches, eat breakfast and get the kids out the door to school. Refer to definition of *pandemonium* for more context.

7:30–8:30 a.m.: Exercise. It could be at the gym a couple days per week, an at-home workout another day, or hiking the trail near my house.

9:30 a.m.–3:30 p.m.: Work. We'll keep this broad for now. This is where I batch together daily activities with my business.

From 3:30 onward, the kids are back home. There are sports some evenings and errands to run. Did you catch the amount of time dedicated to work? Six hours a day. Thirty hours a week. That's what I have found works well for this season of motherhood and entrepreneurship. I choose to work on my business while the kids are in school.

It's true. I could add back an extra two hours per day if I forwent exercising and showering afterward. By forgoing the exercise, productivity levels are likely to fall. Actually, let's rephrase that. They *will* fall. Exercise is a stress release that's critical because stress is a major inhibitor of mental clarity. You need mental clarity to show up ready to create, to learn, to be as productive as possible in the amount of time that you have. Think of it this way, in simple terms: Exercise creates energy. Energy increases productivity. We can disagree and still be friends, but I'm telling you that exercise allows me to produce more in a six-hour window than I could produce in a seven- or eight-hour window without exercise.

As I write out this schedule, I can think of dozens of interruptions and exceptions. You will too. No two days are identical. Projects, events, goals, and life in general will dictate flexibility in your schedule and require you to make adjustments other times. The purpose of this exercise is to put a generic, yet ideal, schedule together that you'll begin to craft your day around.

Test me on this. I know you're arguing with me that if eight hours a day is too tight as is, how would six hours work? I can tell you exactly how it works. You get right to work. You focus, you adhere to your schedule, and you don't take a bathroom break every half hour. If you don't have time for it, you make a choice as to whether it really needs to happen or not. If you can't squeeze it in yourself, you delegate it to someone else or to a website or program that does the work for you. Remember earlier when we talked about the 80/20 rule and agreed that 80 percent of productivity comes from just 20 percent of the time we put into it? What does that really tell you? It tells you that there's a whole lot of fluff, sis, that you don't need to be doing. It tells you that maybe you'll begin to prioritize differently, maybe you'll realize you need to delegate more, and maybe you'll kick the habit of second-guessing your every move because you no longer have time for it.

Chapter Takeaway

Before moving on to the next chapter, jot down your ideal schedule. Ignore all of the excuses and reasons that you feel you can't adhere to it or that clients will still interrupt it, and focus in on the realistic block (or blocks) of time that you know you can give undivided attention to your work.

Unlearning Your Own Story

"Hi, honey, I know you're so busy, and I won't keep you, but I just wanted to tell you …"

My mother-in-law begins every conversation this way. Some people start a conversation with "Hey, how are you?" but she begins with an apology for interrupting my day. It used to drive me nuts, and not for any reason other than it told me there was a perception that I was too busy for her. It bothered me that I was somehow responsible for creating that narrative for her. Honestly, I wouldn't have answered the call if I was too busy for her. I know who I'm answering the phone to, and I'm well aware of the average length of the conversation I'm about to embark on. She's one of those women you can call to ask a simple question, and that question somehow turns into a deep, unrelated conversation. It's the rabbit hole that you go down and come back up—albeit a half hour later—feeling better than you had before the call. I'm aware of this, and I consciously choose to answer her calls.

Despite my attempts to tell her that I willfully stay on the phone, she still knows that I am a busy mama of two with a growing business and side projects that account for every waking moment of my day. Just like anyone else, though, I'm in control of my day. Granted, for years, I said yes far more than I should have. I said yes to volunteering almost weekly in Dakota's classroom. I said yes to putting both of my girls through a preschool with school hours that were less than ideal for a working mom rather than putting them into a full-day preschool. I said yes to managing a half dozen rental properties and overseeing multiple flip properties as they were acquired, remodeled, and sold. I said yes to running a business with my husband. I was in control of the decisions I was making yet no one understood how I managed. As I would tell my mother-in-law time and time again, "I'm never too busy for the things I *want* to do. I make my schedule, I answer the calls I want to, and I can make room for anything that matters to me."

So where's the disconnect? It's the same disconnect that we have with one another. We can't fully understand a reality that is different from our own.

Hers Is Green, Mine Is Red

Do you have that woman in your life who just seems to carry so much on her plate? The one who you sit back and can't understand how she does it, why she does it, or what void she's trying to fill? I can't prove that she is or isn't filling a void or that she's handling everything as well as you think she is. Your reaction to what she's pursuing is influenced by your own lens. Your perception is based on your life, your experiences, and what you deem as a balanced schedule. If you're in a season of life where you're stressed at work and exhausted from the very moment you wake up in the morning, then seeing someone juggle multiple projects and three kids without looking like she's aged ten years in the last six months can seem unrealistic. Our perception of others is shaped by both our experiences and our insecurities.

I once hosted an enneagram workshop for women attending a networking event. My friend Angie, who had moved out of Arizona a couple years prior, had reached out to me about putting together a workshop for women to come and learn more about all of this enneagram stuff we'd been hearing about. She was coming into town, and we agreed it would be a great draw for the networking events I'd been hosting. Angie was able to illustrate a perspective that helped me understand why it is that we struggle to relate to one another or understand how another woman can do something that we seemingly cannot.

Thirty women sat in their white folding chairs in a semicircle of the small venue that evening. With her southern accent and adorable skinny jeans, Angie introduced herself and began to explain what drew her to becoming certified to teach workshops like this. She explained that this study of personality traits had been organized into nine different categories. Through a series of questions, you would then be given a number that assigned you to a personality type. This is known as your enneagram number.

"You and I are sitting in the same room right now. There's no disputing what's in this room, who is here, where things are placed," she said. "Imagine that I'm holding up a transparent green sheet in front of my eyes right now. It's my lens. I can still see everything in this room, but everything I see is a varying shade of green." We all nodded in agreement. "Imagine that you're holding a similar transparent sheet in front of your eyes but that it's red." Our heads slowly began to nod up and down, our brows furrowed as we realized where her analogy was taking us. "We both see the exact same room. The same people, the same pieces of furniture. But I see it in shades of green while you see it in shades of red. Neither of us are seeing anything incorrectly, just differently."

Angie went on to explain that that was how she liked to introduce enneagram. We all see the same world, situations, and people around us, but we each view from our own lenses. In the case of enneagram, they break them into nine different groups (or lenses, as I like to think of it). I thought of my mother-in-law in that moment. When she thought of my average day, she saw it through her own lens. Through her lens, my life looked busy, perhaps even overwhelming. Through my own lens, a different color than hers, my schedule seemed very much in line with what I desired.

Think of the person—whether you know them or not—that you often compare yourself to. While you truly shouldn't concern yourself with what *she* is doing, you need to be reminded that there is so much beneath the surface that you're unaware of. You don't know what she's delegating, what she's feeling, or how much time and effort has gone into what you're seeing on the outside.

For my mother-in-law, her experiences were far different than what mine have been. Decades ago, she married my father-in-law and left her job at the bank she'd been employed by for an entire decade. She stopped attending college and worked toward creating their new life together. For the next two decades, her purpose was found in raising two sons, keeping a home, and caring for the needs of her family. When the boys were grown, her purpose shifted as she began designing, making, and selling porcelain dolls from a room she had converted into a crafting studio within their home. She was very successful creating one-of-a-kind, exquisite collectible dolls. She opened a doll-making business right out of her home and sold each one for thousands of dollars. Nowadays, she spends a couple days per week cuddling and immensely loving on her three grandchildren in that crafting studio. With each changing season of her life, she has found her purpose and poured herself into it.

Her view of my day-to-day is interpreted through her own lens, the lens shaped by her own experiences and decisions. The same would be true if you looked inward at my life, or if I looked at yours. We can't comprehend what we don't experience or resonate with. A life for one person might be more slow-paced, while another may thrive in a fast-paced lifestyle. This is no different than someone that lives in a rural town compared to a city dweller. Neither is right, and neither quite understands the appeal of the other, but it works for the person whom it allows to thrive.

My mother-in-law has learned that I can show up as the mama to her grandbabies that they deserve, and frankly, while my life might be quite a different version than what she has experienced, she respects it more than I could've ever imagined. She lent an unbiased ear to hear my heart when I told her that I was going to *be* the example of the woman that I encourage my daughters to strive to be someday, rather than settling for less than what my heart desires. It didn't matter to her that my path looked a little different than hers. I was beyond surprised when she supported my mission to reach other women who were chasing kids and chasing dreams. You know why I was surprised? Because I was trying to guess her perspective from my own lens. My lens might be blue. Hers might be green. And yours might be yellow. Remember that the next time you look at the mama across the table from you. Encourage her in her journey, tell her to keep her chin up and what you admire about her. She could use it—I guarantee it.

Know What Makes You Tick

Most people expect productivity to be a list of hacks, statistics, and best practices. There are definitely systems, tips, and tricks that can help you become a more efficient person, both personally and professionally. We'll cover some of those in the next chapter, but we have to stop and acknowledge that all of the productivity hacks in the world aren't going to help someone that lacks self-awareness and adaptability. Earlier, we talked about exercise needing to show up consistently in your life in order to create energy, which in turn increases your productivity. It's mindset and commitments like that, that will allow you to increase what you do while scaling back the effort that it takes to get there.

Let's go through a couple of examples so you can see what I'm referring to with self-awareness, for starters. As I wrote the manuscript for this book, I began to notice that I couldn't get near the amount of words written if I sat in my home office as compared to a small, quaint coffee shop a few miles down the road. It's contrary to what you'd think. My home office is where I ran a business with my husband for over a decade. By working from home, I was able to avoid distractions and eliminate a commute, for starters. My plate was so full of tasks and emails that a home office was the perfect space for me with that business. No one was knocking on my office door to ask a question; no one was asking me to grab lunch or gossiping at a water cooler. When I shifted careers, I began to realize that there wasn't a plate of eighty tasks in front of me anymore. Instead, it was a blank, white sheet staring back at me. I was no longer in a response type of mode like I had been for all those years prior. As a writer, you're on the front side of things, creating the concept, outline, stories, and emotion that a reader will feel. I found myself having moved from one end of the spectrum (responding to things as they came up) to a career in which I was the one needing to create something for someone else to respond to.

Do you know what you're apt to do when you're sitting at home, trying to think of where to begin? You turn into a squirrel. I would stare at the screen, let my mind wander, and search for a story for the chapter I was working on, and then get up and throw a load of laundry in the washer or make another cup of coffee. Neither of those things began to spur new thoughts or get me further in my writing. They just became easy-to-go-to distractions. I had hoped that inspiration might strike me as I sorted clothes or poured the last drop of creamer into my coffee. It never did.

Being self-aware of my squirrel-like tendencies, I packed up my laptop one day and drove down the road to a little coffee shop that had recently opened. In the middle of the coffee shop, there's this grand, rectangular community table (the kind where several strangers sit next to each other). It's carved out of a piece of wood, smoothed to a glossy shine on top and wavelike outer edge. I rose on to my tiptoes to slide on to the barstool and set my laptop on the table. I grabbed the tangled white earbuds from my purse and turned on Pandora from my phone. While there was hesitation that I could write with earbuds in, I knew that I would otherwise get distracted by the two high school girls gossiping on my right. There I sat for the next three hours, writing until I hit my word count. I couldn't get up and distract myself. I was forced to think through old stories in my head, to type, delete, and start over until I finally had a chapter completed in front of me. In the most unlikely of places, this writer had found a way to silence the squirrels and narrow her focus.

Put the Big Rocks in First

Think about your most recent to-do list that you wrote and cheerfully crossed off as you went along. Your list likely had one or two big items— whether that means they were urgent or really time-consuming—and then a slew of smaller tasks that you insisted on writing down. Which tasks did you complete first? Chances are, you started with the quick and easy items like putting away laundry, writing a social media post for your business, or reading your emails. Yes, those things needed to get taken care of—I'm not disagreeing with you. However, I'm willing to bet the big item or two on your list were taken care of near the end, or maybe they're still sitting on your list.

The big projects take more time, focus, and require you to be fully present. We often tell ourselves that if we rid of all the small tasks, then we'll eliminate the interruptions when we go to work on that bigger project. Sure, it makes logical sense when you put it that way. But listen, I can promise you that you'll never empty the list to where you eliminate all distractions. There's always going to be everyday things to knock off the list. As fast as you cross them off, you add in new to-dos. The good news is that those smaller items aren't going to keep you from achieving what it is that you're chasing if you ignore them for a bit. The bad news is that those smaller items are going to keep you from achieving what it is that you're chasing if you continue to attend to them first every time.

On Sunday afternoons, I grab my weekly planner from my office and head over to my little corner of the couch in our family room. I should probably mention that there's only one feature that I insist upon in a weekly planner: the layout. The layout has to show me my entire week when I open it up, and more importantly, it has to break out my day by the hour. Small, empty boxes the size of a quarter aren't enough to plan out your week. If the traditional calendar with thirty bite-size boxes is all you have to work with right now, then I highly suggest grabbing a blank piece of paper instead. Write out your entire day hour by hour until you can run over to a store and get yourself a more productive planner. We aren't chasing miniature dreams, so let's not limit ourselves to miniature boxes as we plan out how you're going to get where you need to be. When I open my planner to a new week, there are appointments blocking out an hour here or there that I have already put in, but for the most part, there are chunks of a few hours at a time with the open space to define what that day is going to look like.

You might not be an entrepreneur, or maybe you're building your business or passion project while you still keep your nine-to-five. You're not alone in that. If that's the case, I'd encourage you to look at this two ways. When it comes to what you're creating outside of your normal day job, focus on the blocks of time available either before or after work or maybe even during your lunch hour. In regard to your day job, you might want to break out that eight-hour day as well. The more efficiencies you can find, the less stress you have depleting the energy that we already talked about you needing for this purpose-driven project you're building.

Back to the planner. Most sane people will just leave the empty spaces empty. While I still consider myself sane, I have come to learn that leaving an open space in my week can just as easily be filled with an impromptu coffee date with a friend or, you guessed it, crossing off the ridiculous little items on the daily to-do list. Instead, I take a glance at my entire week and start to fill in the "big rocks," as I call them. The big rocks are the non-negotiable, big projects you have. They're also the moments that are really important to you, like eating dinner with your husband and kids most nights or exercising at the gym four times per week.

You have control over what your week looks like. As much as it can feel like your clients dictate your schedule or that things can unravel pretty quickly you will surprise yourself at how much is within your control if you set the boundaries upfront. When I work with clients, I stress this topic over and over. They have control over their week. You have control over yours. As an entrepreneur, you have a tendency to be overaccommodating, and it's easy to understand why. You're the sole source of income in your business (at least in the beginning), the only person to answer the phone and emails, and the only person creating the product or offering the service. If you're closed and unavailable at a time that a client is requesting, you run the risk of losing the business altogether.

Please understand that I know this story through and through. My husband and I were the overaccommodating, always-available types. I've always been an early bird and would be able to respond to clients as early as 6:00 a.m., while my husband would start a little later and respond until, say, 6:00 p.m. If I was making dinner, at the gym, or doing school pickup rounds, he was there for coverage with our business. When he left the office, if someone called or emailed, one of us would respond—8:00 p.m., 9:00 p.m. It didn't matter. We always responded.

I had to call to make a doctor's appointment for myself the other day. The receptionist answered, politely asked me a few questions about what I needed to be seen for, and then said she was pulling up the schedule. She asked me if a couple of times would work for me, but they did not. She asked what an ideal day and time would be. I told her Friday's worked best for me, and she quickly said, "Oh, we can't do Fridays. The doctor isn't here on Fridays."

Well, I thought, *that's what I wanted but I guess I need to figure out a different day.* After hearing another option or two, I booked an appointment with my doctor.

Why is your business any different? Why are you in fear that if you don't clear your calendar for every client that calls in that your business is going to suffer? The phone call to the doctor's office was the reminder

I needed that clients want to work with the person providing the product or service. Clients call for all sorts of appointments, and they adhere to the office hours, the availability of the business owner or employees, and then the clients (not the business owner) shift their schedule to receive the product or service. Think about other places you regularly make appointments with: hair stylist, dentist, CPA. All of them will tell you the available times, and you choose what fits best. When you're the client, you adhere to the business's schedule. Your business isn't any different than this, so start giving your schedule the boundaries that you want for it.

It feels counterintuitive, I know, but take it from someone who has tried and tested this. In my coaching business now, I offer appointments on certain days of the week and at certain appointment times. Period. Outside of those days and hours, I'm focusing on the other big rocks in my life.

With your planner in hand and the week within view, begin to write in your top priorities for yourself personally and professionally for the week. Write in the days and times that you will work out at the gym. If you don't figure out when you can go to the gym on a particular day, it becomes very easy to pencil in an early-morning appointment instead. Do you remember when we talked about being self-aware earlier? You know the big rocks in your day-to-day. Put them in there so that when Wednesday at 10:00 a.m. rolls around, you know exactly where your attention needs to shift to.

Same Rocks, Same Jar

There's a reason I chose the analogy of the big rocks for the important aspects of your day-to-day life. I once listened to a speaker, a middle-aged man with a southern accent, and watched as he walked across the center of the stage to a small round table. He had a large glass vase that sat empty in the middle of the table. Next to the vase, he had a smaller glass jar filled with sand and several rocks on the tabletop—each rock about the size of the palm of your hand. As he began talking, he described distractions and busyness that our lives are filled with as he poured the jar of sand into the empty vase to illustrate the time that is taken up by each of these time suckers. He put the empty jar down and picked up a large rock as he began to compare it to the important aspects of our lives: a date with your spouse, quality time with your children, your work, and so on. With each example, he would put a large rock into the vase. The audience watched as the rocks began to pile atop the sand and then on one another. The vase was filled to the brim, but there were still a few rocks sitting on the tabletop, illustrating that we don't make enough room for the important aspects of life when we fill our vase with small, tedious and unimportant things first.

The speaker began to remove the big rocks and set them back on the table as he talked about crowding our schedules and our lives. When the rocks were out, he poured the sand from the vase back into the original jar it had been in. He picked up the rocks and began to put them into the vase, one after the other. Sitting in the audience, I remember thinking that we already knew it wouldn't all fit. I wondered where he was going with the point he had seemingly already made. When he finished putting in all the large rocks, the vase was full. There were empty spaces on the sides since the large rocks didn't fit like Tetris pieces within the vase. The vase appeared full nonetheless. He picked up the jar of sand and began to pour it over the top of the rocks. It seeped down the sides and crevices of the big rocks falling in between them, below them, and on top of some of them. When he finished pouring the entire jar of sand, the vase was full, but not overflowing.

You cannot argue with the demonstration, nor can you argue with the analogy. If things aren't fitting right now, then what do you have to lose by at least putting priority on the items that matter most to you?

No Secret Sauce

If you spent the next six to twelve months reading at a ferocious pace, attending workshops and conferences, or seeking advice from a mentor, you'd come to realize that there are no secrets in business. What the mentors and speakers are doing isn't something you can buy. And that's the good news. All they've done is tap into a mindset that has removed barriers. They have hyper-focused on their vision or purpose and created a day-to-day that allows them to pursue their goal at a healthy pace. Productivity is two chapters in this book for a reason. We'll cover the strategies in the next chapter, but you first had to adopt the shift in mindset. It sounds woo-woo, I know. I was that person once too.

Both my husband and I have been asked over the years to go to dinner or get on a conference call with friends and colleagues. "I just want to understand how you grew your business and what I can duplicate into my own," they say. And you know what? We've been happy to meet with them. What many expect to hear is that there's a specific thing we did that changed everything. Spoiler alert: there isn't. We put our heads down, worked really hard, and then invested in ourselves. Investing in yourself is tough to do until you wrap your head around the fact that you're gambling on *yourself*. We aren't talking about throwing money at a machine, closing our eyes, and then peeking out of one eye to see what happened. No, we are talking about the most strategic investment you could ever make: *yourself.*

If you're stretched too thin right now, investing in yourself is the only move you have. You're at a glass ceiling, and until you decide to punch through it, you're going to have to make a choice: dial things back or continue treading water. Investing in yourself could be as simple as hiring a house cleaner, or hiring a sitter to pick up and watch the kids after school. Do you remember when I told you earlier that people couldn't understand how I was managing so much at once? I didn't lie and tell them I was doing it all on my own. I told them, for example, that someone cleaned my house. That saved me a couple of hours every week, and I was able to make more in a couple of hours than what I was paying the cleaner. There's a very clear ROI on that. We also hired a high school student, Ashley, to pick up our girls from their schools (they were at two different schools with different pickup times back then), bring them home, get their homework done, and burn a little of that crazy energy off of them. Again, with the amount we paid Ashley, I could make far more in that amount of time than what I was paying her. More than that, though, I could come home as Mom. I didn't walk back into the home office when I got home. Instead, I walked in the door with a smile on my face, started making dinner as the girls climbed up on the barstools at the kitchen island and told me about their days, and then played a game of Sorry or Uno after dinner. The rate of return was far greater than the cost of paying a nanny for a couple of hours a day during the week. It also turned the late afternoons into quality time. I was present and more balanced.

Investing in yourself might also mean hiring a coach, purchasing software, or hiring an employee or company to begin to alleviate your workload. This is often a much tougher investment, but it's still an investment in yourself. True, you could be hiring your first employee, and it feels as though your investment is in them, not you. Ask yourself why you hired the person in the first place. You knew that by freeing up your time and delegating X, Y, and Z to the new employee, you could focus on the aspects of your business or project that would allow it to grow. You're allowing yourself to be productive with the big rocks, not the menial tasks. That's an investment in you. Do you see it now?

Why Free Advice Often Doesn't Translate to Real Results

When I first began offering business consulting, my go-to clients were Realtors. Though I had never been a Realtor, coming from the world of residential mortgage loans meant that I worked with Realtors very closely and understood the intricacies of their day-to-day. Before I had ever even thought that I was someone that could offer business expertise to others (my head was too far into our own daily pile of tasks), my husband and I had been approached by a Realtor who wanted advice on how to scale his business the same way we had scaled ours. He'd watched us over the years and wondered how our volume increased, how we managed to afford to pay a new employee an annual salary, and then how we could hire another person and then another. For an outsider, it piqued a tremendous amount of curiosity.

Brandon was far too busy and asked if I'd take the meeting. Unsure of what on earth I was going to tell our friend, I showed up and listened. He asked questions, and I answered earnestly. I shared the raw feelings, risks, mishaps we didn't even know to anticipate, and triumphs when things finally fell into place. I shared the marketing strategies that worked, the ones that flopped, the software we'd invested in, and the business coach we had hired. I was an open book without an agenda. While the Realtor left that conversation with loads of information to sift through and consider, I left with a realization that years and years of experience, trial and error, perspectives, and risk tolerance had all accumulated into a database of knowledge that I could share with others. Beyond that, I realized that the knowledge transcended industries—the business principles, the mindset, and the inner drive that Brandon and I had tapped into was something we could guide others through.

After that conversation with the Realtor that afternoon, a funny thing began to happen in the months that followed. A handful of other Realtors, none of whom knew about the conversation I'd had with the first guy, reached out with similar requests. The excitement of helping them make a breakthrough in their own strategy was reward enough for me at the time. The idea of turning these meetings into a new business hadn't yet become something I was ready to pursue. Instead, Brandon and I were paying $15,000 a year for formal business coaching, spending countless hours and big money on our own business to test strategies and implement new systems, and then sharing those findings with these business partners that were reaching out to us.

Want to know what happened with a handful of those partners that specifically asked for those informal coaching sessions though? Not much. If the advice were lacking in those meetings, I wouldn't share this piece with you, but this illustrates the importance of investing in yourself far greater than any other example I can give you. You see, when Brandon and I invested thousands into coaching and then thousands more into marketing services, client appreciation events, and hiring additional team members, for example, we received tangible results. Our business continued to grow year after year. With every check that we wrote and handed over, we acknowledged that we were committing to show up bigger than we felt capable of—or else we may as well have thrown the cash into a fire pit. There's a huge difference between cutting a check to a business consultant, listening for an hour, and then showing up two weeks later compared to the person who cuts a check to the same consultant, listens for an hour, and then implements every single thing that was discussed in the session. Does it surprise you much to hear that when I offered *free* advice—the same advice that we had been coached through for the prior couple of years and that had increased our sales volume by millions—the recipient of the free advice never acted on it?

They didn't act on the advice because their wallets weren't tied to what happened next.

Chapter Takeaway

Go online and search for enneagram tests. There are simple, free tests available online. Some websites may have a small fee associated with their more comprehensive test and may include the ability to connect you with a certified expert or trainer as well. Taking an assessment to identify your personality traits and tendencies is a great start, but take it one step further. Ask your employees, executive staff, or spouse to take the assessment as well. Understanding the viewpoint of those that you surround yourself with or make decisions with is imperative to the future success of your relationships and your business. Remember when we talked about investing in ourselves? Well, friend, I was nudging you toward bigger investments, but why not start easy? Start by investing time (and perhaps a small fee) into self-awareness and awareness for those that you're doing life (and business, possibly) with every day.

Design Your Productivity Formula

When I had our first daughter, Dakota, I can remember an old woman (whose face I cannot remember, but her words—well, I remember them often). As I held my newborn in my arms, she said to me, "Oh, you know what they say about having little girls, don't you? Little girls steal their mother's beauty."

Alex, can I get Things People Say to Make Others Feel Less-Than for 500, please? Seriously. It should be a Jeopardy category. I'm not even kidding. I'm not sure what the reaction on my face was, but I was thinking, *Are you saying I look ragged?* Is this supposed to somehow make me feel good? What reaction is this woman expecting from me? Despite the insert-foot-now commentary coming from this woman's mouth, I knew that things were different. I wasn't necessarily thinking that I needed to fret about my appearance—I was twenty-three years old! As far as I could tell, I still looked like I was in my twenties.

Okay, but some things were definitely different even if my appearance hadn't yet gone downhill. Life as I knew it had flip-flopped seemingly overnight, and I had to find new ways of dealing with things to try and create the reality I was used to. Despite having once been a bartender in college and working until 2:00 a.m. and then waking back up at 8:00 a.m. for a nice morning hike—well, that was different. Dakota could have me up until 2:00 a.m., but the next morning didn't start at 8:00 a.m. My chipper morning persona had been replaced by a messy bun atop my head, complete fog brain, and an oversized shirt with milk stains down the front of it. It was glamorous, let me tell you. (On second thought, maybe our babies do steal our beauty for a bit.)

The antidote to my newfound nocturnal life? Coffee. So much of it. What else? Well, happy hours with my girlfriends fizzled out because I couldn't drink or be gone too long (unless I had managed to pump enough beforehand). But, boy, did I miss the socialization. My new happy hour became the hour-long group fitness class I signed up for at the gym.

All kidding aside, I wouldn't change the lack of sleep or the life turned upside down for anything. What I subconsciously began to learn though was that every time life shifted, I needed to make a shift as well. To bounce back to my hyper-productive state (albeit, with another human at my side), I needed to create a new normal. New habits. New scheduling. New normal. We each find ourselves in similar situations at some points in life even if not because you become a new parent. The issue? Sometimes, you create a new normal that will inevitably backfire on you. With more responsibility and the same amount of time, we begin to juggle. We begin to multitask. Then, we begin to fall apart.

That's Not Going to Work in the Long Run

You're an incredible multitasker, I'm sure. You're able to rock a baby to sleep while listening to a podcast and brainstorming your next social media post. Yes, I also know you can cook dinner while checking and responding to emails and take a sales call without the potential client having any idea that you're doing those other things. I know because I've been there. I know about the checklist you write out (where you include the things you already did, just so you can start the list with some momentum by crossing off the first and second items on the list). The issue isn't the checklist. The issue is how you handle the checklist.

Here's where you're going to want to argue with me. Honestly, I wanted to argue with myself for agreeing to put this next statistic in the book. You are actually about forty percent less productive when you multitask. You end up with half-finished projects, you aren't laser-focused, and your work just isn't as creative as it could otherwise be. Forty percent less productive.

That wasn't what we thought when we bragged about multitasking, was it? No. We thought we were being forty percent more productive, didn't we? It felt that way, but it was just the excitement and energy we drew from the dopamine, really.

Multitasking is something that women do much better than men. Knowing how well we multitask is likely why women wear it as a badge of honor, to be honest. Multitasking, though, is the fast track to burnout. It's the sign that we aren't giving enough attention to the things that will give us the real momentum we're seeking.

Now, as a recovering multitasker (and one who easily relapses), I'm not suggesting that there's a way to get around how much we have on our daily checklist. I know the real world. I know you need to buy groceries, get the oil changed in your car, take your daughter to dance class, schedule a week's worth of social media posts, and squeeze in twenty client appointments this week. I know. What I am suggesting, however, is that you take the big projects and approach them a little differently this time around.

Batch like a Boss

Batch work is the antidote to multitasking. Think of batching much like meal prepping. You might be making an entire week's worth of lunches—maybe even dinners too—at one time. For those focused heavily on what they're eating and portion sizes, this is an incredibly effective way of staying on track. For a few hours of your day, you aren't doing anything other than grilling chicken, steaming vegetables, and portioning out meals into Tupperware. When you're finished, your entire week of lunches and dinners are totally done.

Batch work can give you the unrushed chunk of time in your calendar to focus solely on one thing. Think of next week and what your business might need. Regardless of the type of business, it's possible that you need to make a product, ship it, create and post content on Instagram, Facebook, Pinterest, and the list goes on. Perhaps, your line of work requires that you create videos, blogs, or podcasts. Your day might include making sales calls, returning emails, or meeting with clients.

What if you set aside a chunk of time—maybe an entire day

(depending on what it is you're working on)—and focused solely on that one thing? Hopping back and forth can be exhausting. You might start the day responding to emails, then stop halfway through to take a client appointment. When you finish, you return to the emails. From there, you shift your focus to packing products that you need to ship out but stop before you're finished because another appointment arrives. Do you see how disruptive and choppy this approach is? It can crush your creativity. It can make you less productive with the time lost trying to reacquaint yourself with where you left off and get the momentum going again when you move from one task to the next.

In theory, batching this is a great solution, but the reality is that many businesses operate in a mode of chasing urgencies and inviting chaos into their day-to-day. You may not be able to batch every aspect of your business, but you can certainly find some things to rearrange and alleviate your schedule. This might mean you shift your appointments to being done only on Tuesdays and Thursdays. You might set aside three hours on Wednesdays to write as many blog posts as you can. You aren't focusing just on that week's blog post and moving on. No, you're sitting there, and if you come up with three blogs, then you just put yourself ahead by three weeks. Get it? Imagine if you took a couple hours on Fridays and batched the entire upcoming week of social media content. Preplanned content gives you the added bonus of avoiding the face-palm moment when you realize you forgot to post today. If you have a podcast, you're scheduling multiple interviews in a single day to get as far ahead with content as possible. What does batching look like in your business or project?

The reality for some businesses, though, is that they can't batch a lot of the menial tasks. Look for the projects, the things that will make your business move. Batch the brainstorming session, the design work, the time spent creating or making the product, and the social media marketing campaigns. We'll address alternatives for those types of businesses next.

Delegate the Small Things

You don't have to batch everything, nor can you, really. As much as I know meal prepping would be a time saver for me throughout the week, it's not my jam. I can't grill dozens of pieces of chicken, pounds of broccoli and brussels sprouts, sort them into containers, and then eat them for the next five days. Okay, I could. I just don't want to. Not everything you do is something that you'll want to batch. It really depends on your field and what your typical days consists of.

Divvy out the menial tasks that are important but easy to train someone on. For a growing business, the investment in hiring a new full-time employee might be too big of a leap. Consider hiring a high school or college student part-time. Ask a family member if they'd be willing to help. Offer an internship to a student. Hire a third-party company that specializes in redundant tasks such as sending out gifts, writing and mailing thank-you cards, creating and executing email campaigns, sending out prerecorded voicemails, sending and managing texting campaigns, or creating marketing material. All of these things can be created upfront and managed by an entry-level intern or employee. Start small. Remember: the more you can delegate, the more you can free up your time to focus on the revenue-generating activities that allow your business to grow and serve more people.

One of the most common things I hear from clients is, "I know I need to hire and delegate, but I'm just so busy right now. When I have some free time, I'll definitely look into this." Can we be real for a minute? There's never a perfect time for this. There's never going to be a moment that you want to briefly pause your momentum in order to find, interview, hire, and train someone. You can make it a little easier on yourself, though.

1. For one day, write down every task you do. Responding to emails, answering calls, writing out thank-you cards, shipping products, creating social media content, sales calls, meeting with clients, the list goes on.

2. Evaluate the list. What if you could get back two hours of your time just by simply having someone else respond to email inquiries and phone calls or by packaging and shipping your product?

3. When you identify what tasks can be delegated, you begin to design the new role. How much time might these tasks take on average? What are the steps to completing each task? The next time you sit down to do these tasks, write out a cheat sheet that the

soon-to-be-newest member of your team can reference to shorten the training time you'll need to invest into them.

Narrow Your Focus

As you've been reading through these chapters, your mind has been swirling with ideas. You're homing in on your purpose, your vision, and how you're going to put it into motion. Inevitably, you're going to find that you come up with multiple avenues to get to the same goal.

When I first replaced myself in the business that Brandon and I had grown together and shifted my focus to building my new company I asked myself a series of questions:

- ☐ Where do I want to be in three years?
- ☐ Where do I need to be in one year?
- ☐ What do I need to do right now in order to get to my one-year goal?

Reverse engineering the vision is a great starting point. It forces you to take the large-scale vision of who you want to become and to strategize the steps to get there by breaking it into smaller, measurable check-in points. There's a common caveat in this process that I want to bring to your attention. Though the process is intended to narrow your focus, you'll often begin brainstorming many options when you get to the third question. This is normal, and mapping out multiple possibilities is a great way to visualize the various paths you can take. The key is to pick just one path, though, not all nine that you end up with on your whiteboard.

When I created my company, I knew that there were certain obstacles that would come up that I would be able to push through much quicker than others because I had built a business before. Many of the barriers that I had encountered in the prior decade had taught me lessons that would allow me to grow that much quicker this time around. There was one aspect I misjudged, however. I thought that because of my experience and knowledge that I could build multiple platforms all at once. During the first year, while I was still hiring, training and transitioning out of the business with my husband, I sought to build Meant for More's platform as a blog, a book, a nationally-traveling speaker, and podcast host. I hesitated to even admit that in this book but felt so compelled to warn you against this mistake. Am I saying that a business cannot have multiple platforms? No. It absolutely can and you can scale to that, but focus on one endeavor at a time in the beginning. When I began to realize I was wearing myself thin and not progressing as planned, I refocused my efforts. Meant for More started as a blog because transitioning out of a business was very difficult to do and took time that I couldn't push fast-forward on. As that transition began to wrap up, the business grew to offering business coaching and small networking events. It then shifted— when the timing was right— to publishing a book and focusing on guest-podcasting and speaking engagements that enhance the book's underlying message. It couldn't be rushed. It had to organically grow. The same is true for your business and ultimate vision.

When you look at other businesses and see them managing multiple projects and platforms at once, just remember that the inertia that got the business off the ground took a tremendous amount of time and effort. Once the momentum was going, that freed up time and energy allowed that business to then begin to focus on other endeavors. With delegating, hiring, and focusing on efficiencies, a business continues to free up more resources to take on additional avenues.

You Aren't the Solution

With any business, whether service- or product-based, you're going to start out on your own, more than likely. In the early stages, you're responsible for everything from providing the actual service (or creating the physical product) to finding potential clients, creating a marketing funnel and sales pitch, to marketing on social media channels, to creating the entire process that a client goes through from first interaction to becoming a client to the end of the transaction. As your business grows, it's increasingly difficult to release the reins on any aspect of the business. Something as menial as writing thank-you cards can feel worrisome that the same attention to detail may not happen if you were to delegate the task to an intern or new team member.

This is where a shift in mindset is absolutely necessary. If you were to grab pen and paper and write out the journey that a client of yours takes from the first social media ad they come across through the time they purchase a product through you and leave a review at the end, you may come up with thirty individual steps—who knows, maybe far more than that. You've created a business with such intention and attention to detail that you meticulously create the journey that your clients experience. When doing so, though, you often shape a narrative in your own mind that the client is expecting each step to be from *you*. This can hinder many entrepreneurs because as they grow, so does their workload. The idea of growing a business and scaling back the time that you put into your business is a far-fetched concept, right?

I know how frustrating it can feel to work tirelessly only to find yourself in the same spot months later. They say that change is the only constant, yet change is exactly what most of us try to avoid. Instead, embrace it. Embrace the journey. Embrace the face-planting decisions and flops along the way. Once you've narrowed your focus to the one item you are going to pour yourself into, consider incorporating it into your morning routine. Whether it's just thirty minutes or an hour, any bit of uninterrupted time where you can focus on that one item is going to be better than juggling eight different projects that move at a snail's pace.

Chapter Takeaway

Spend time answering the questions discussed in the chapter to clearly align your vision with your day-to-day efforts toward that goal:

1. Where do I want to be in three years?

   _____

2. Where do I need to be in one year?

   _____

3. What do I need to do right now in order to get to my one-year goal?

   _____

Crafted to Sell

After college, I went to work for a very large bank as a financial advisor. I thought I'd be one of those kids that went into the industry that she obtained her degree for. Don't feel bad if that same plan didn't work for you; it didn't last long for me either. I was green, but I now had a degree and several licenses that advisors were required to hold in order to trade stocks, mutual funds, discuss life insurance products, and give someone advice on where to invest their hard-earned money. Our country had just entered what was being called the Great Recession, and the major news stations focused solely on the stock market and unemployment rate day after day. Many of the calls I would take were from concerned clients who thought if stocks went down they would never go back up. They found themselves caught up in the media headlines and didn't know what to do with their retirement accounts and investments. "Sell my shares," was what I heard on the other end of the line for the majority of the calls that came in from the time I arrived in the morning until I clocked out at night. Like other new grads in the financial industry, we found ourselves learning by immersion into a recession that none of us had experienced or could fully grasp yet.

Occasionally, I would get to have a different type of conversation with clients: life insurance. It's the foundation of every single person's portfolio. If you're breathing, you should have life insurance—at least until your assets have grown enough to where you no longer need insurance. One day, there was a call from a young woman that I'll never forget. It's the only specific phone call I can remember to this day from my time with that bank.

"I'd like to look at getting life insurance," she began. "My husband just died, and we are expecting our first baby. I don't know if he had life insurance, but I need to make sure I have coverage in case anything ever happens to me."

Whoa. So many thoughts raced through my mind. *When did he die? How did he die? Did he have a policy to protect her? Wait, that's why she's calling me. I pray I have good news for her.* She went on to tell me that she was expecting a daughter in April and that her husband had been struck by a bus and killed instantly. My eyes had welled with tears, my hand laying softly on my belly where my own firstborn was growing inside of me.

The bank had a policy in place that whenever someone called in to report a death that they were to be transferred to a particular department that handled these types of situations. As her account information came up on the screen in front of me, I could see that her husband had a $400,000 life insurance policy in place. She was the beneficiary. I couldn't tell her myself. At least, I didn't think I was supposed to be the one to share that. I knew I had to route her to that other department so that they could share the details of the policy. I explained this to her, but she calmly asked that we finish putting together her policy first.

Though it was a conversation that probably lasted less than fifteen minutes, it's one that resonated so deeply within me. In college as well as in obtaining my licenses, it was reinforced that life insurance is the base of your portfolio. It protects your family and your assets when the unexpected occurs. After the conversation with the young expectant widow, I carried her voice in my mind. With every portfolio review (that's where we look at a client's assets and where their money is currently invested or not invested), I looked for life insurance. Whether they wanted to listen or not, I knew I held the licenses and was much more well-versed in financial well-being than they were. It was my responsibility to lay out the information, guide them in the right direction and let them make a decision from there.

The bank I worked for offered two types of life insurance at that time. One was called *term insurance*, which is coverage for a set amount of time like ten or twenty years, for example, and is the most inexpensive type of insurance. A husband and wife might each carry a $500,000 policy for twenty years. At the end of the twenty years, the insurance is gone. If they pass away during that twenty-year period, the policy would pay out the $500,000 to the beneficiary. Pretty straightforward type of policy. It's inexpensive because the odds of someone passing within a set period of time are pretty low.

The other type of insurance was *whole-life insurance*. That's a guaranteed payout since it lasts until you pass away. Given that the insurance company knows they'll have to pay out the insurance someday, the cost is substantially higher. My personal opinion? I preferred to educate clients and recommend term insurance, so long as they were then investing money at the same time. The idea behind this type of approach is that by the time your term-life insurance is set to expire (let's say it's twenty or thirty years), the money you'd been investing during that time should've grown as well. The need for that insurance policy for your family would no longer be there, hypothetically, if you'd been investing and saving all along.

Several months had passed since I had taken the widow's phone call, and my manager pulled me aside one day. "We just got the companywide reports for sales, and you're number one for term-life-insurance sales. Out of all of our advisors in the country, you have the highest number of sales for term insurance."

"Wow, I wasn't expecting that!" I said, with a huge smile on my face. I thought back to the young widow. I knew that was the moment that as an advisor it became about more than sales for me.

"Yeah, so great job on that, but, uh, we just want to help you grow with selling other products. Your numbers on whole-life insurance are pretty low. The company doesn't really make much money on term. I'd like to help you balance that out a bit."

Wait, what? Did he just compliment me and tear me back down in less than thirty seconds? I didn't quite know how to respond to him. I bit my lip and looked down at my hands as I thought about how to respond to him. After a moment, I looked up. "I understand there's not much of a profit margin with term insurance, but I can't recommend something I don't believe in."

My manager sighed. I began to get the feeling that he needed me to bend, but he could tell that I needed convincing. "Steph, tell me what you need to work through in order to sell more whole life."

"I'm not sure what to say," I began. "I just don't agree. It's my licensing, and I need to stand behind what I recommend, don't I?" I understood where he was coming from as a manager. I really did. At the end of the day, though, I refused to budge.

Selling only works when you can come across as if you're not selling. The only way to do this is to believe in what it is you sell, represent, or offer as a service. If you don't have an emotional connection to what it is that your business offers, then don't expect a potential client to have one either. As we'll dive into more in this chapter, you'll see that buying behavior is led by emotion. Your ability to create emotion will ultimately drive the trajectory of your business.

The Story Creates Emotion

Long gone are the days when a business card or flyer could convert a prospective client into a paying customer for you. Nowadays, we are exposed to an estimated four thousand ads per day. Some reports suggest it's actually far more than that. Between social media, billboards, commercials, people we interact with, and every product containing logos and taglines, we live in a saturated world of products and services. Marketing and branding create a white noise that we learn to tune out to avoid being overstimulated by everything we come across. The brands you recognize and remember are the ones that do something different. They capture your attention and find a way to stand out amongst the other 3,999 ads you saw that day. Do you know how they do it? They craft a story.

From the time you were born, you were told stories. Fairy tales, fables, and family stories that you retell to your own children now. At a young age, we're introduced to movies that do the same thing. There's an incredible book that every business owner needs to read written by Donald Miller called *Building a Story Brand* that details the seven components that every memorable story contains. You can think of any book or movie and clearly identify each component that he talks about. As he explains, every story has a *character*, who encounters a *problem*, and then meets a *guide* who gives them a *plan*, inevitably leading to a *call to action* when things reach a climax, resulting in *success* and *avoiding failure*. I'll leave the summary this brief because I want you to read it for yourself. It's *that* good.

Now, the components aren't the *aha* moment when creating a story. No, the secret to effectively using a story to support your brand, your nonprofit, your sales or your passion project is the role you choose to give *yourself* in the story. So often, we want to be the hero. Donald talks about this a great deal and reminds us that we aren't the hero. Not in the story you're telling anyhow. Sure, you might be a social media ads manager that can increase sales and conversions for your clients' businesses and you're thinking, *Yeah, that makes me a hero! I can increase their sales! How am I not the hero?* but it's to your detriment if you position the story this way. Those ideal clients don't want to hear you talk about yourself. They don't want to see themselves as a supporting character in *your* story. What fun is that for the potential client? Instead, if you position your ideal client as the main character (the hero, if you will), then they begin to imagine themselves in the story you're telling. Suddenly, the story is about *them*. Now, you have their attention.

So where do you and your business come in? After all, we are trying to help you increase sales and conversions here. You and your business are woven into the story intentionally as the mentor, the chaperone, the director, or as Donald Miller puts it, the *guide*. Picture yourself at a coffee shop with your ideal client. You're taking a sip of your latte as she begins telling you about this issue she's struggling with. You almost choke on your coffee as she gets midsentence because you realize you can totally solve her issue. As she sighs at the end of her dilemma, a huge smile comes across your face as you reach over and tell her, "No, no, no. Don't stress. I can absolutely show you how to fix that."

You begin to outline the steps she would have to take, be it two steps or twelve, to get to where she needed to be. Can you see her face looking back at you? She's overcome with relief. She's so grateful for this coffee date and for the advice you've just given her. She's ready to proceed and to let you lead her to the solution, the solution that your business offers. Did you notice that you didn't tell her that *you* could fix it? No, instead, you told her you could show *her* how to fix it.

Now, it would be amazing if every client fell into your lap like that, but the reality is that they won't, right? Instead, you have to create that story so that it attracts your ideal client. Creating the story is reverse engineering the journey your client takes from their first interaction with you, your post, or your ad all the way through the purchase and use of your product or service.

My shampoo shows up in my mailbox like clockwork. It's a subscription-based company. It sounds weird when I say it like that, but nonetheless, the shampoo and conditioner arrive at my house every other month. The problem that this particular shampoo solved for me is not something I can find in another shampoo at Target or Ulta. Maybe I could rephrase that last sentence. If there is a shampoo at Target or Ulta that *can* solve the same issue, then that shampoo company hasn't told me they can solve my issue yet. See the last part of that sentence? "Hasn't told me about it yet" is the key phrase in why a story needs to be crafted. Oftentimes, consumers (myself included) aren't aware of the problems we have that need to be solved.

Amazon reminds you that you're too busy to go to the store. Uber reminds us that taking a taxi is much harder than it needs to be. Walmart reminds us that stuff at other stores are expensive. Each of these companies position the problem that they want their target audience to identify with. See, once you and I identify with a problem, we're committed to the rest of the story. We're watching the commercial and thinking, *Yes! Finally, someone gets it. That is so me!* as we watch the rest of the commercial. We see the character follow through with a couple of steps and voila! Their problem is solved.

When we see ourselves in the story, the emotional connection is made. When you identify with the character, it becomes your story. The problem becomes your problem. The steps you watch the character take become your own action plan. The company or the brand are positioned as a footnote when stories are crafted correctly. The story isn't about them or their accolades, but it is instead about the problem that resonates with you. The companies that succeed in storytelling are the ones that show you how to solve a problem you have, even the problem you didn't realize you had in the first place.

Finding Your Niche

A couple years ago, I can remember talking to my younger sister on the phone. It was the late afternoon, and I had just walked out of an appointment with one of my coaching clients. As I got in my car, I pulled the buckle over my lap and grabbed the shifter to reverse out of the parking spot. It shifted into reverse as I glanced back over my right shoulder, and then I put it back in park. I turned back toward the steering wheel and reached for the phone to call my sister, Natalie.

Do you have that person in your life whom you'll call with an idea even if you haven't worked the entire thing out in your head yet? No conversation is off limits with Nat. Some conversations are as lighthearted as a hysterical meme that she wants to tell me about, while some carry the stress of us having a father in early-stage dementia. Other times, we swap stories of what our kids just did. (Most recently, she called to tell me that her boys began hitting golf balls in the backyard—that story ended with a $700 window replacement for her neighbor.) It's never a dull conversation for Nat and me. Truth be told, I can open up with my husband just as much as I can with her, but when I need to ramble on for a long period of time and talk in circles, I turn to my sister. Nat isn't afraid to tell me when she disagrees or when she thinks I've lost my mind, and she doesn't hesitate to celebrate the victories with me either. She's one of the most genuine people you could ever meet.

I had called Nat to see if she had proofread the very first blog I was going to publish.

"Hey, did you read that email I sent over to you? I'm scared to hit publish. Is it too vulnerable?" I asked.

"I read it last night after the boys went to bed. I thought it was inspirational for moms trying to raise kids and build careers. Totally got me teary-eyed at the end when you talked about *being* the example for the girls, though," she said.

"Did it resonate, though?" I asked. Nat and I are incredibly different, and at that time, I thought that getting her opinion on things would be my best shot at constructive criticism. I could beta-test material on her, and if she didn't understand or if she disagreed, I could go back and revise to make my points clearer.

"Well, I choked up because I knew it was you and the girls, and I could feel your emotion behind the words. But, honestly, Steph, it's just not me. Maybe it's that I'm not a risk taker. Maybe it's just that I don't have any big dreams. I don't know. I think someday I might, but right now. It's hard enough just to get them off to daycare, work all day, and get them in and out of the bath before bedtime. I just try to get through each day."

I wanted to debate her in that moment. I wanted to tell her the potential I saw in her, that it was okay to dream and have a vision for her future, but I didn't. In that moment, I chose to let it be.

I'm sure you've had a similar conversation with someone before. You pour your heart out and they look at you with a blank stare. You share your why, and they can't relate. It's okay when that happens. In fact, it should happen. If you've crafted your story or nailed your elevator pitch, then it should resonate with a specific audience. Your story, your product, and your service are created for a specific type of person. You aren't running a grocery store, so we don't need to attract everyone in a five-mile radius of you. In that moment, I recognized that Nat could be supportive of me even if she didn't quite share the same feelings.

My sister is not my niche. In fact, my sister-in-law, my mom, and mother-in-law aren't either. If those closest to you don't understand what it is you're pursuing, why you're investing in yourself, why you dream as audaciously as you do, or what drove you to start your company, it's okay. Maybe they do understand what you're chasing after, but it just isn't for them. They can watch from afar, and they can cheer you on regardless. If they don't cheer you on, that's okay too.

Finding your niche isn't a difficult thing to do, but it will make all the difference in how you talk about your product, vision, company, or passion project. Your niche is your ideal customer. If you close your eyes and picture yourself sitting across from that customer, what does he or she look like? What are they wearing? What do they drive? Are they married? Do they have kids? What kind of job do they have? Where do they hang out in their free time? Do they purchase high-end, or bargain shop? How old are they? Do they find services and products on social media, or by window shopping? Are they well-educated in your area of expertise, or are they someone looking for guidance? There are dozens of questions you could ask yourself. You want to narrow in on this person as specifically as you can.

Pay close attention to the big-name brands around you. Take, for instance, Target and Walmart. They both offer the same types of things. We can categorize their products as "everything." Who is their target audience? Some might say, "Everyone, of course!" While we all need toothpaste and socks at some point, neither of these retailers attempt to win all of us over. Both are megastores that offer us everything from groceries to crafts to bedding to bicycles, but they don't market themselves alike whatsoever. Walmart brands themselves as being the place to go to find low prices. Target, on the other hand, doesn't try to compete in the price arena. Instead, they market the latest trends and market to women. One is appealing to the customer who's more concerned about finding the lowest price of dish detergent. The other is appealing to the woman that wants a plant-based dish detergent option.

As someone who mentors female entrepreneurs, I once had the same fears that are swirling through your head right now. You're worried about directing your messaging too specifically and losing traction with the other potential customers, right? I worried that by not broadening my message to both men and women that I was losing out on a huge piece of the market. The reality is that the more generic my messaging was, the less I had the ability to resonate with anyone at all. I couldn't write or speak the way I wanted to. I couldn't use the examples that really helped me make my point because only half the audience would likely understand them. The more specific your messaging is, the more you stand out, the louder your message then becomes, and the clearer you become to your ideal customer.

There's a decent chance that you might be your ideal customer. Many times, women start businesses as a result of trying to solve a problem for themselves and, in turn, create a business out of it. If that's you, then you know exactly what makes your client tick. If it's not you, then start to narrow in on who it is that you're going to be talking to. The more you can visualize your ideal client, the easier it will become to craft your message and speak directly to them. Remember: we're flooded with four-thousand-plus brands per day. Unless it sounds like someone is speaking directly to us, the message is lost in the white noise, isn't it?

They Don't Know the Problem

Your messaging, your sales pitch, and your marketing material isn't about you. We've covered that. Your business exists to solve a problem and to serve your clients. You might remember earlier in the chapter when we talked about buying behavior being driven by emotion. The quickest way to evoke emotion and to resonate with a person is to put a problem in front of them. You want them to listen and immediately think, *Yes, that's me!* When people can identify themselves as the character in the story you are telling, you have their attention. Keep in mind that the problem you are aware of, the one you know how to solve, isn't as obvious to the person that experiences that problem. It sounds counterintuitive, but oftentimes, we need to call out the problem to grab the attention of those who really resonate with it.

The problem becomes the hook in the story you're telling. Think about some of the products or services that you purchase. Do you use a specific type of coffee creamer? Why? You might use a nondairy creamer because you have a sensitivity to regular types of creamer. What type of car seat did you buy for your child? Was it the most reasonably priced, or did you choose it because of the safety ratings? Do you go to the movie theater, or do you rent from Netflix? Your answer might be based on wanting a night out where you can put on real clothes and splurge on eighteen different flavors of popcorn. When you're ready to sell your house, do you call a real estate agent, or do you seek out the real estate investment firms that offer to buy your home from you? Your answer might be based on wanting to fetch the most amount of money for your home, while others might be looking for the quickest process. In all of these scenarios, as well as any type of ad that you come across, there's a problem that they offer to solve. The problem is going to narrow their niche and give them the best chance at converting someone into a paying customer.

Chapter Takeaway

Evaluate your website, your ads, your emails and your messaging. Are you positioned as the hero, or are you creating a story that your ideal client can see themselves within?

Audit your messaging:

1. What problem am I solving for my client?

   _____

2. Does my messaging tell the client what the problem is?

   _____

3. Is my messaging focusing on my business or on my client?

   _____

4. Do I have a clear call to action for the client to engage with me?

   _____

Failing Forward

I looked over at my husband sitting on the dark-gray couch in our business coach's office. He was nodding slowly, his eyes slightly squinted, deep in thought as our coach talked to him about scaling back his hours in the office. His nod indicated his agreement, but I knew all too well what he was thinking. He was nodding as if to suggest that the idea, in theory, was great but that it would never work. It was unrealistic. It was a pipe dream. In Brandon's mind, if he was working nine or ten hours a day, five days a week, and taking calls throughout the weekend and evenings as needed, then how was there ever a world in which he could set his own hours? More importantly, how do you avoid losing clients if you scale back your availability?

Brandon's stress levels had been elevated for years. He had become mentally entrenched in our business as it grew over the years to the point where he couldn't stop. He couldn't stop taking phone calls. He couldn't stop the day's activities from racing through his mind at night. He couldn't flee the toll that stress was taking on his body. I was waving the proverbial white flag *for* him. I wanted to wave it for myself too, but I needed him to change his approach if we were going to continue to lead our business together. While our marriage was very much intact, my instinct knew that we couldn't continue working at the level we were working at. We had a hard time working together throughout the day and then changing the conversation completely as soon as the clock struck five o'clock. It's a very conscious decision to be on the phone sorting through a decision or problem with your spouse one moment and then talk to him fifteen minutes later about what to make for dinner or what time you'll be home from the kids' soccer practices.

Our ambitions were losing the joy they had brought us before, and we dreamed of enjoying our lives in a more meaningful way with our two little girls at home.

Something had to change.

It's incredibly tough—despite what anyone will tell you—to run a business with your spouse. There are times that it's exhilarating. There are moments when you might go to lunch together or drive to meetings and appreciate the fact that you're in this adventure together. That is absolutely true, but there's another aspect that you don't hear people talk about. There are decisions that have to be made, especially when you decide to punch through the glass ceiling and grow the business to uncharted levels, and it isn't likely that you're going to agree on every aspect of it. Imagine having tough conversations and trying to find common ground with a business partner. It can get awkward, stubborn, or uncomfortable sometimes, right?

Now imagine at the end of the day, sitting at the dinner table together, going to the park with your children, or driving to a family function when you've just disagreed on a major investment or direction for your business. For us, it didn't create strife in our marriage. We have always worked intentionally to separate work and our marriage, but there are times that you can't easily turn off the conversation. There are emotions, there are decisions that need to be made, and there are fears and conversations that need to be had. Just because you turn off the light and walk out of the office doesn't mean that it isn't still weighing heavy on your heart. There are times that we had to continue to talk through decisions at the dinner table, or late at night when the kids went to bed. Likely because of me if we're being honest. My husband has a much easier time removing emotion from decisions and keeping a level head. I'm driven by emotion and have always struggled with needing to plan twenty steps ahead before I'm willing to make drastic decisions for our future.

He and I are very much believers in seeking a mentor or coach—an unbiased person who can put eyes on your goals, business, and strategies—to guide our business. Though our business had grown significantly with just the two of us playing a continual game of trial and error, we were both open to the possibility of what an outsider would see when they looked in at our business.

So there we were, sitting in our business coach's office facing the reality we'd found ourselves in: overworked, on the verge of burnout, and still chasing an even bigger vision for our lives and business. Brandon couldn't conceive the likelihood that he could work less and still sustain our business and the employees that relied on us. He knew from colleagues in our industry that it was possible, but logically, it didn't make sense yet.

As with most people, drastic change can be overwhelming. As I mentioned earlier, Brandon was nodding his head in agreement as our business coach told him he needed to drop to a four-day workweek immediately. There was a giant whiteboard to my right, and as I began to drift in thought, I could see the blue dry-erase marker slowly writing Brandon's excuses on the board in my mind. I could see all his objections without him having to verbalize a single one. I had already worked through them in my head. I believed that we could not only sustain our business but ultimately grow it to much higher levels and scale both of us back to some extent. The problem is that we both had to buy in on the idea. If we didn't, then scaling back on my own hours was only going to mean one thing: Brandon would increase his hours to compensate for me scaling back.

Sometimes, decisions will be made for us. Not making a decision is the same as making a decision. Within a couple weeks after that meeting with our business coach, the decision had been made, but not by Brandon or myself. It was an October morning, our kids were on Spring break from school, and I had just woken up to start packing our SUV. We were headed to Disneyland that morning, so like any trip that we take, I was up before Brandon and the girls to pack snacks, double-check the luggage our girls had packed themselves (three stuffed animals in lieu of socks or underwear for my seven-year-old), and write a note for the house/dog sitter that would be heading over.

"Steph, can you come in here?" Brandon called from the bedroom. I walked in, pushed the thick, navy drapes back to let the light in through the glass door to the backyard, and looked back at him. "I can't move. I tried to sit up, and I physically can't," he said.

I didn't say anything. I just stared at him. *Was this like the man-flu type of exaggeration? Sounds a bit extreme. I mean, who can't move all of a sudden?*

Neither of us realized the extent of what had occurred. We called a friend of ours, a chiropractor who lived nearby, figuring that Brandon must've thrown out his back. We made plans for him to see the chiropractor after the swelling subsided enough to have him shuffle down the hall and into the back of the SUV. At the chiropractor's office, we discussed him flying out to meet us in California the following day. With the plans in place and tears streaming down our faces as we pulled out of the driveway, I drove the girls and myself to Disneyland. The next day came, and my husband hadn't improved enough to meet us. The third day came, and he called to tell me that he wouldn't be flying out to meet us at all. With each phone call, I begged him to let me drive home. There was a sternness that I hadn't heard prior to that moment and haven't heard again since, when he told me that we couldn't come home. He admitted that things hadn't improved since the girls and I had left and that he'd been sugar-coating the severity to keep me from a complete meltdown. A minor back injury had transpired into a full-blown autoimmune response within his body.

Over the weeks that would follow, he would only be able to move about gingerly. His weight plummeted twenty-plus pounds within a few weeks. His muscle mass began to deteriorate, and the resilient spirit I had always seen within him had been dulled. When he finally returned to his office, he could sit in a chair for a couple of hours at most before the pain would become too unbearable. His own body and physical pain forced him to leave the office after only a few short hours each day. The team, me included, had to quickly adjust to figure out who was going to do what and how to keep things moving to accommodate Brandon's limited capacity for the foreseeable future.

The decision that had been presented to him weeks earlier had been made *for* him.

After seeing a handful of different doctors, all testing came back negative. The internal inflammation, the presumed autoimmune response that remained nameless—none of it had an actual diagnosis. At the turn of the year, about three months into this still-unexplained injury, Brandon began to slowly increase his time back in the office. He had a very long road ahead of him, answers to seek, strength to rebuild, and a decision to make again. This time, *he* made a decision. He decided to create a new normal consisting of only four days per week in the office.

A year later, I walked into the bathroom as Brandon was getting ready for the day. It had taken ten months for him to regain most of his strength, weight, and muscle mass. He was eating clean, juicing almost daily, and trying to work out about four days a week. I sat on the side of the bathtub, my hands folded in my lap, and looked at him through the mirror.

"Do you know what today is?" I asked. He glanced over at me through the mirror and nodded. "You know, the whole thing is surreal, isn't it? There was never a diagnosis. It really makes you wonder why things happen. As awful as it was for you this last year, maybe this is opening up space for something more for you."

We've all had setbacks in some area of our life. For one person, it's the product launch that absolutely flopped. She lost her entire investment in it. For another, the setback might be the fear of leaving her stable, salaried position to pursue her own business. For yet another, it's feeling like an utter failure of a mother when you forget to pick up your kids on a half day at school (guilty on this one on more than one occasion). As much as each of these situations—isolated—can be rationalized and learned from, the issue is that they add to a narrative that's already in your head.

Do you remember the two different voices we talked about in chapter 1? You have one voice in your head that tries to give you a little push, to think bigger, to act bolder, and to open your eyes to the opportunities around you. She's the girl that adamantly tells you there is a bigger plan at work. The other voice, though, she's the kind of girl you don't invite to brunch with your girlfriends. She's negative and would probably have stolen your boyfriend in high school. The latter one, that's the voice of a girl who will continue to tell you that your setbacks are the very reasons you should give up. She'll tell you you're dreaming someone else's dream, that you don't have the resources, the platform, or the connections to bring your vision to fruition. She's only right if you listen to her.

It's only when you stop trying that you can call it a failure. If you try again or make some slight adjustments that take you slightly farther than the last attempt, well, then you have inertia. You have forward momentum. This is what I call *failing forward* and failing forward inevitably leads to success. The difference between those who succeed and those who don't is the resiliency of the person making the decisions.

It's All in the Roots

There is an old Chinese tale that I once heard about a bamboo farmer. This farmer successfully grew a variety of crops year after year. One year, he decided he wanted to try something different and introduce a new crop—bamboo. The farmers around him weren't growing bamboo, but he had researched how to cultivate the crop and set out to do so. He planted the seeds and watered them daily. Weeks and months went by, but not even a tiny sprout rose above the ground. He continued to water them, despite the fact that nothing was happening. An entire year went by.

The other farmers in the area mocked him and couldn't understand why he was still watering the dirt. Another year went by. Then another. The farmer was still watering the dirt faithfully, and again, still no sign of a single sprout through that entire fourth year. To the other farmers, this poor farmer had lost his mind. He had wasted good dirt, water and four years of what could've been successful crop seasons in their eyes. In the fifth year, though, something happened. One day, the bamboo plants pushed through the surface of the dirt. In the coming weeks, they grew incredibly fast, some towering ninety feet tall!

All this time, the farmer had been faithfully watering without any actual proof that the bamboo would grow. He remained consistent. See, what this farmer knew was that growth had been occurring, just not above the surface. He understood that in order for these bamboo trees to tower to their full ninety-foot-tall potential, they had to grow immense roots below the surface first. The infrastructure below the surface had to be created in order to sustain the magnitude of what would eventually come thereafter.

All of the time and energy you're pouring into life right now—the classes you're taking at night after a full day of work, the forty-five minutes you're moving your body at the gym, the marketing material you're creating late at night after the kids are tucked in—those are all the roots you need in place before you are ready to reap what is in your future. Keep in mind that the bigger your ambitions, the more depth you're going to need in your root system. I often talk to women who feel that their lives are incredibly chaotic, out of balance, and lack any forward momentum whatsoever. They feel as if they're treading water rather than swimming toward any possible shore at all. While that might be true for some aspects of your life (remember, a *yes* to one thing always requires a *no* to another), bear in mind the tenacity of the woman you're aiming to become. The woman you will be in a year is going to face tougher obstacles and bigger decisions. The work you put in today is for the woman you become next year.

There is a scripture that I came across that has the ability to speak directly into the soul of the person—man or woman—that is questioning whether they will ever reach the goal or purpose they set out for. Proverbs 16:9 (ESV) says, "The heart of man plans his way, but the LORD establishes his steps." This one statement has the ability to humble you and pick you up off the floor at the same time. For the proud, it's a reminder that ultimately, He is in control. Not you. Not me. For those feeling defeated, it's a reminder that sometimes the tough seasons of life are meant to shape us into the person we need to become to fulfill our purpose. I often remind myself of this verse when I think back to the long, painstaking path that Brandon has been on since that October morning when he couldn't get out of bed. Might it be that Brandon's steps had to look a little different (than otherwise planned) to get to where he ultimately wants to be?

You Had to be Molded First

One Saturday morning, we pulled up to the soccer fields for the girls' games. As Brandon opened the trunk of our SUV to begin unloading the chairs, the girls grabbed their bags and raced each other to the entrance gate. Given that the girls had no idea what fields they were playing on, I grabbed my coffee and went into an awkward jog (the kind where you're trying to run but you don't want to spill your coffee) to keep them from getting lost in the ant farm of children running everywhere. As I caught up to the girls and redirected them toward the game field, we passed an old neighbor of ours. I gave her a tight squeeze and lifted my sunglasses to the top of my head.

"Catch me up. I want to hear what you're up to these days," I said to her. As our kids ran in circles nearby, I listened as she told me about remodeling her kitchen and having been laid off from her job a few months prior. With the layoff, she decided to make a career change and was heading out of town for training a few weeks from then. The smile on her face told me that she was in a good place. She was content with where she was headed, and quite possibly more excited than she had been before the layoff even occurred.

"Okay, your turn. Tell me what you have going on. I'm subscribed to your blog and need more details on what's to come," she said as she turned the conversation back to me. I spent the next couple of minutes emphasizing the vision of the blog and the speaking engagements.

She sighed. "Steph, that sounds amazing. I'm so excited you're pursuing all of this." And then she ended the statement with a surprise. "It's too bad you couldn't have started this years ago. Imagine where you would be by now."

For a split second, I wanted to agree with her. It would've been amazing to start years before, and already be on the other side of the challenges that every business endures, but I shook my head and reminded her, "I wouldn't have been able to do this years ago. I would've been speaking on topics I hadn't lived through. Those years and that business are the expertise that no one can take from me. It's my credibility."

Understand that the idea in your head and burden placed on your heart can come to fruition, but the timing of it and the precise path are not entirely within your control. I've met countless women who have started down one path, ambitious and completely dedicated to their job only to walk away years later. They change careers or pursue something they could've never envisioned years before. There's one common denominator with every single one of them, though. The person they needed to become was shaped in those prior years. You might be able to visualize right now who it is that you want to be, what you want to provide to others, or what you want to create, but you cannot truly understand the depth of what it will take—and who you need to become—in order to fulfill that dream.

Chasing Cheese

Like any journey, there are going to be twists and turns. You will find a routine, gain momentum, and then things will be interrupted. It could be in the form of competition, technology, the economy, or something else completely out of your control. Your ability to adapt, to change your approach, or to completely redesign your business model is what is going to allow you to impact others in the way that you were intended to. The end goal will remain the same. The goal doesn't have to change. The path to get there, however, may have to.

In college, one of my professors assigned us to read the book *Who Moved My Cheese?* by Dr. Spencer Jordan. It's a super short book written as a parable about two mice and two small people that live within a maze. Day after day, the main goal for the mice and people is to navigate the maze and find the cheese. The mice and people both find the cheese. To no one's surprise, the cheese is moved one day. The mice quickly adapt and find the cheese again in its new location. The people, well, they struggle. They keep thinking it will reappear in the same location and have quite a tough time adjusting to a new normal. They had taken the cheese for granted and are very slow to adapt and find the cheese again. Despite the book being a parable, it isn't too far-fetched is it?

Every industry is impacted by change, be it from technology, a recession, or the people whom you are used to doing business with. When you find your business reaching a point where you begin to coast—things are running smoothly, the routine is in place, the sales are coming in—that is when you want to be most aware that change is on the horizon. If you're willing to adapt, you'll come out the other side of the change and have a stronger business and vision than you did beforehand. If you resist the change, cover your eyes, and pretend it hasn't come, then you'll very likely lose traction and begin to fade.

Failing into Success

In 2007, a junior in college at the time, I was laid off from my full-time job with a mortgage company. I had a mortgage of my own, a new vehicle, student loans, and credit card debt. The year 2007 was the dawn of the Great Recession, as we now refer to it, and being in the industry that I was in, the effects were felt about a year sooner than for everyone else. There were zero mortgage companies hiring. They were all doing layoffs. Though other industries were still hiring and oblivious to what was going to be facing them in the coming year or so, I was keenly aware of one fact: my lifestyle relied upon every dollar I was making at my prior job. I could take another job, but I was going to have to sell my home and my car. I wouldn't be able to find a position that was as lucrative as what I had become accustomed to. Not as a junior in college. Not as someone entering a new industry at entry-level.

When I tried to sell my home, I became hyperaware of the shape the U.S. economy was in. Home values were dropping like I'd never heard before. In college, we had studied recessions and stock markets, but this wasn't in the textbook. This didn't make any sense whatsoever. The home I had purchased in 2006 for $240,000 from a homebuilder was now selling for about $150,000. The home builder was trying to finish the last one or two streets of the neighborhood my home was within and had slashed prices to essentially remove any profit margin whatsoever—just to sell the rest of the inventory, I presume. They were in panic mode over what was going on. It was catastrophic for homeowners who were now immediately impacted by these new home values, and found themselves laid off of work too.

With no job and a hefty mortgage, my hands were tied. I couldn't sell my home. I called the mortgage company and asked them about a "short sale" at the recommendation of my Realtor. He had explained to me that a short sale is when a homeowner sells their home for less than what they owe the mortgage company. It has to be approved by the mortgage company since they're taking a substantial loss and not receiving a full payoff of the original loan. Feeling a sigh of relief that there was a possible option, I called my mortgage company to ask for approval. The representative at the bank said, "I'm not sure what that is. A short sale? I don't think we do those. Sorry."

You and I both now know that short sales took place all over the country during the Great Recession. Unfortunately, my request was just a little too early. By the time I was ready to graduate a year later, I had lost my first home to foreclosure, returned my vehicle to the bank (because that, too, wasn't able to be sold for what I owed on it), and had a new job earning about half of what I had been earning previously.

I was humbled to a point that I will never forget. Under the advice of an attorney, I also filed bankruptcy. The concern at the time was that I might be susceptible to the loss the bank took when they sold my home at auction (which only sold for about $100,000). Legislation was later passed that protected tens of thousands of Americans who all went through similar situations, and bankruptcy wouldn't have been necessary in the long run. However, it had already been filed long before the legislation took place.

There I was, twenty-two years old, with the worst financial track record you could imagine and walking across the stage to receive my bachelor's degree in finance. Though I was ashamed at the time, I reflect on the irony with a chuckle today. How? Because when you fail forward, you grow. When you grow, you find a silver lining in the dark seasons that you've been able to crawl your way through.

So why share my biggest failures with you? Well, why not? The person I became thereafter was shaped through humility and through navigating really difficult times. For the first couple of years, I couldn't get a car loan or even a meager five-hundred-dollar credit card. I was forced to create a new normal, a normal that didn't mirror that of my colleagues, my friends, or even my family members. The hardships that you live through will ultimately mold you into the person you need to become for the next phase of your life. Your behaviors become disciplined. Your decisions become more carefully planned. The problems you previously had fret over become so minimal that they aren't worthy of your worry.

When you are at your worst, God is at His best. When you realize that your ability to control a situation is fabricated, only then are you ready to allow Him to take the reins. You listen, you pray, and you open your heart to answers you couldn't hear before that moment.

Life is going to test you. Even when you home in on your purpose and you begin to create the passion project or business that you feel called to build, the tests will continue coming. Embrace them. When you've wiped the tears away, close your eyes, bow your head, and clasp your hands together. Thank Him for the trials knowing that He's allowing them only because He needs to shape you into something far greater than you realized for the task He has set on your life. Find the silver lining and acknowledge that the situation could have been worse and express gratitude for that. By doing so, not only does He see the difference in your heart, but your mind distinguishes the difference as well.

Chapter Takeaway

One of the most powerful exercises I have done personally as well as with clients I've coached is to create a timeline of the events that have taken place in your life. This begins with the absolute earliest memory you have. You may have been three years old, and if so, that's fine. Write it down. As you write out the timeline, write each event and memory in either the positive or negative column. Keep the events in chronological order. Don't try to balance the sides. Don't overthink the events. Grab a few sheets of paper and set up your timeline similar to the below example. You may choose to revisit the timeline over the course of a couple of days as your memory is jogged.

Once completed, take notice with the negative events. Do they have a similar theme, a common person or place tied to them? What about the positive events? Do they have a similar person, workplace, city, or location tied to them? Do the positive events seem to occur before or after the negative events? Are they related at all? The pattern will begin to unfold only as you take a step back and begin to look for commonalities in each column, or cause and effect that you may have never realized previously.

Have your biggest triumphs come after a failure, tragedy, or misjudgment? Had the negative events never occurred, can you attest with certainty that you would still be the same person today? Let's find your patterns and identify the silver lining in your story thus far.

Timeline

Positive	Negative

Changing Direction Midway Through

Sometimes, the lives that we write for ourselves are ones that we wish we could erase. Every single one of us has those moments; others have entire seasons of their lives. *Why couldn't our lives be written in pencil?*

See, that's the beauty in each of our stories, though. Yes, we have mess-ups. Yes, we have chapters that are formed from a season of life, and those chapters might be dull. They might be messy. They might be full of tears and angst. The beauty of those chapters, though, is that they aren't the ending of your book.

Think about it. The best books engage us, take us on a journey, bring tears to our eyes and laughter into our soul. This next chapter—the next phase of your life—doesn't have to be a new career. Do you remember when I introduced you to Andrea, the girl who wanted to take a mission trip? She didn't leave her job or the country despite what she originally thought she was being called to do. Instead, she found a local mission to feed, clothe, and serve the homeless. Her purpose wasn't about her career or a particular place in the world. It was about fulfilling a desire to serve others. This next chapter of yours doesn't have to be a continuation of a prior chapter either. For you, this might mean new friendships. It might mean moving to a new city. It might mean changing your business plan halfway through the year. Give yourself permission to change direction when the need arises.

Waffles for Dinner

I finished typing the last sentence, sent the email, and shut my laptop. With my eyes closed, I took a deep, five-second inhale as I reminded myself that I needed to transition from work back to Mom and tend to the chaos that I could hear down the hallway. I opened my eyes as I let out the long exhale and stood up from behind my desk. I could hear the girls laughing and screaming as they played tag down the hall. The dogs were barking and chasing the girls as they ran. I didn't have the energy left to walk into the room as a fun mom nonetheless put dinner together and start to double-check homework folders. I was completely exhausted from yet another day of stressful client conversations and an endless list of tasks.

As I walked into the kitchen, I opened the refrigerator to see what combination of protein and veggie I could scrap together without too much effort- or too much complaint from the kids. Nothing looked good. I shut the doors and stood there for a moment.

"Dakota, grab the waffle maker," I called.

The girls stopped chasing each other, looked at one another and then over to me to see if I had a brief mom-brain moment, or if I had suddenly morphed into a really cool mom. Breakfast for dinner wasn't a norm in our household, hence their confusion.

"Grab it," I repeated as I looked over at her. "We're doing waffles for dinner. Who wants to help me?"

As much as I had been trying to drown out their loud shrieks of excitement up to that point, I smiled when they both let out an enthusiastic scream and jumped up and down in that moment. They ran over, hugged my waist, and then began to pull out everything we'd need to make breakfast together. I stood back and watched as the girls attempted to measure out the right amount of waffle mix, spilling just as much onto the countertop as they got into the cup. I smiled as they both tried to stir at the same time—waffle mix had made its way onto their cheeks and had somehow landed on the dog's head below them too.

"Mommy, do we still have to eat vegetables tonight too?" my youngest asked. She had a look on her face as if she'd just swallowed a sour Skittle. I laughed, knowing she was picturing the taste of maple syrup followed by a spoonful of broccoli.

"No, honey." I laughed. "Just breakfast tonight."

That evening could've blended into the week like any other night, but in that moment, I decided to change course. Rather than letting my thoughts swirl around about the day, the tasks and the uncertainties that awaited me the next morning as I cooked dinner, I instead chose to chase after something joyful. There are going to be days, weeks or seasons of your life that test your spirit. One day may bleed into the next. Another day may test your patience, your strength and your abilities. The ability to take pause—to completely pivot our approach in the moment—will replenish your soul when you need it most.

We often get so caught up in living task to task that we forget our lives are predetermined by an hourglass, one that none of us are privy to seeing. With each passing day, do you really want to live your life on a conveyor belt—one that takes us from appointment to appointment and from place to place? Routine is important. I won't argue that. But think about Thanksgiving, for example. As a mom with two kids now in school, every Thanksgiving I think the same thing. *You just started the school year. Like, literally just started. Maybe three weeks ago, right? How is it Thanksgiving?*

No, it hasn't been three weeks, Mama. It's been three months (Arizona kids go back to school as soon as you flip your calendar to August. Long gone are the days of going back to school after Labor Day.) So why do we have such a hard time internalizing the actual amount of time that has passed? It has to do with routine. We wake up Monday morning and instantly fall into a state of routine. We put our heads down, do a little happy dance on Wednesdays to celebrate getting to the halfway point, and then let out a deep sigh on Friday evenings. Is it really a surprise that the weeks fly by when we go into a state of autopilot Monday through Friday?

The only real way to slow the clock (in your mind, at least) is to interrupt it with memories. Skip the gym class you were going to head to tomorrow morning and go for a hike instead. After you pick up the kids from school, without saying anything at all, drive to the nearest fro-yo place in your area. Change it up. If for no other reason than to slow the clock by intentionally creating an interruption, change it up.

Your ability to stray from routine is what will allow you to create the business or passion project you originally set out to create. The excitement you had when you first decided to launch your business will fade as the months pass by. As your business grows, you go from a state of fulfillment within yourself to a state of playing catch-up. In the same way you need to create intentional disruption in your personal life, you need to be nimble in your approach to your business. When you're at your busiest, you're most vulnerable to inhibiting your own growth. Why is that? When you're busy, it's just like the weekday schedule you adhere to.

You're Not a Chameleon

Whether you like the idea of it or not, you're a reflection of the people that you spend the most time with: the women you work out with in the morning, the friends you grab coffee (or happy hour drinks) with, the colleagues at work or the clients you tend to attract, the ladies in your Bible study, the person you're in a relationship with, and yes, even some of your family members. For some people, this isn't something they want to hear. It may give you an unsettling feeling because you start to question whether you alter your personality, opinions, or demeanor when you're around different people. Maybe your sister is a pessimist, or your mother gossips relentlessly. Are you squashing those tendencies as soon as they come up, or are you allowing them to take place? When you're around different groups of people, are you still the same person, or do your habits tend to shift a bit?

The chameleon-like tendencies we often have to adopt in order to fit in with the crowd will either keep you from stepping into who you're meant to be, or they'll have to be shed. The likelihood that your goals are going to always align with your friends' goals are, well, highly unlikely.

I can remember the first year after graduating college. Many of my girlfriends and I graduated at the same time, but our circumstances from that point on couldn't have been more different. With our newfound salaries, we all began to make bigger decisions than we'd been used to, and by bigger decisions, I'm referring to bigger purchases. For one friend, it meant a brand-new car with a car payment higher than her apartment rent. For another friend, it meant shopping sprees every payday for the nicest shoes, clothes, and makeup and the newest iPhone every time a new one was released. For another, it meant extravagant vacations to every desirable place you've seen on a postcard. The one thing we all had in common? Student loans.

I was envious of the vacations, the beautiful car, and all the clothes. I wanted to spend time with my friends, but the reality of the situation was that I couldn't afford to. I was $34,000 in student loan debt with unsubsidized loans that meant my total loan balance was still increasing (or at best, remaining nearly the same) with each payment that I had made. I had the option of minimal payments for twenty years and barely noticing the debit each month, but it didn't sit right (which is probably a good thing because I had just graduated with a degree in finance, so at least financial theories had infiltrated my brain). The idea of being strapped to my loans for even ten years (the shortest term they offered at the time) was flat-out depressing.

Though my friendships weren't contingent on my debt load (for starters, my friends had just as much, if not more, student loan debt than I did), spending time with some of these friends began to pull me away from the ultimate goal I had for myself at that time: getting rid of my debt. I knew it affected me when I was around people that spent money at a pace that I couldn't keep up with, so I began to withdraw from certain parties, trips, and dinners. My circle became incredibly small, but with Brandon constantly reassuring me that we'd have amazing vacations and a nicer car in our future, I instead put every free dime I had toward my loans. It took almost three years of strict budgets and tax refunds to pay off those loans. Our only vacations during that time were to San Diego to sleep on the pullout couch in the condo Brandon's parents rented each year.

Did some of my friendships change during that time? Yes, absolutely. It's inevitable that your circle will change if you're seeking a different direction for yourself, especially one that isn't incredibly popular. Other times, you'll find that you'll intentionally seek out new relationships in order to create accountability or inspiration. As the old saying goes, "It's not what you know; it's who you know." I'd argue, though, that we all have the ability to know the right people. You just have to put yourself into the room.

Ask yourself this question: If I put all of my friends and family into the same room, would they mix well, or would it be like oil and water? Chances are, you'll be left with oil and water—while some might mix well together, others won't. This doesn't necessarily mean that *you* are the chameleon and that you're having an identity crisis (though, I suppose it could mean that too). It could, however, be a sign of growth. You might have your group of childhood friends, a group of friends that you've met through work or networking events, and a group that you and your spouse spend time with together. Inevitably, when you begin to push your own boundaries and strive for more in life, you're going to create an unintentional distance between yourself and some of these groups of people. Embrace the person you're becoming.

There will always be people in your life that are content—be it that they are in a season of life where they want consistency or a season where they need guarantees. They may cheer you on and encourage you just like my sister does for me. Other people might completely ignore what it is that you're doing, and you have to remind yourself—constantly—that what other people think of you doesn't matter. Write it on your bathroom mirror. Write it in your journal. Set it as a daily reminder that pops up on your phone. Whatever it takes to push the concept deep into your subconscious, do it.

You Can Do This Because She Did It Too. And Her. And Her.

I met Megan in the fifth grade. Maybe it was that we were both pint-sized brunettes doing backhand springs on the grass at recess, but we were instant friends and still are to this day. We had so much in common during those elementary and high school days— fanatic NSYNC fans, sharing clothes, and gossiping about who we had a crush on that week. Like many friendships, odds were that we'd begin to spend less and less time together after we graduated high school. Though months would sometimes go by during college—or even after we'd both graduated—without us having a chance to talk, we remained incredibly close friends. We had an unspoken understanding that we were both chasing goals, settling into relationships with our future husbands and trying to figure out how adults functioned in the world.

Megan had gone to college to pursue nursing. Those few years in college were a shifting point for her. She became hyper-focused on schooling and then on her new career as an RN. I can remember taking a hike with her one spring afternoon. We walked along the dirt path and talked about our newer careers, about newlywed lives, about motherhood for me, and about her toying with the decision of going back to school. We had just gotten out of school a few years prior, but she described this nudge she felt to go back to school to become a nurse practitioner. There were plenty of reasons to chase this big goal: no kids yet, she was young, her career would benefit in the long run. The only hesitation I remember her voicing was knowing that it meant pushing off starting a family. Weeks later, she decided to return to school.

As she returned to school for her doctorate, while continuing to work as an RN, she had found stress-relief in working out. She was in impeccable shape and had taken an interest in fitness competitions. Through her competing, and certainly complemented by her schooling, she took an opportunity to begin coaching men and women with their nutrition- teaching them about the macronutrients that their specific body needed to sustain their health goals and thrive. While other nutritional coaches hopped onto the scene around that time, her credibility as a nurse practitioner (and expertise in gut health) allowed her to speak to topics that other online nutritional coaches weren't near as well-versed in.

Ultimately, her business became so successful that she had the option to leave her position as a nurse practitioner to pursue life as an entrepreneur with her nutritional coaching business. The truth is, yes, she could have skipped all the additional schooling and built a nutritional coaching business. The difference, though, is that she didn't. Her path may have taken several extra steps—and years—but the success of her business is tied back to everything she learned on the path that she took. Though her passion had changed, she ended up finding her purpose over time.

I love stories like Megan's. I could write an entire chapter on condensed versions of other women I personally know who chose to take a blind leap toward their purposes despite the safety of their then-careers. I've seen a woman leave a steady salary to create a mentorship program for teenage, female athletes. I've seen a TV personality walk away from the spotlight to create a journal focused on gratitude. I've seen a woman in sales leave her corporate position to enjoy the freedom of being self-employed as a Realtor. I could tell you about the woman who left the commercial flooring industry to write a book and create a community for female entrepreneurs.

There's more to this underlying thread than the pursuit of purpose. These women rejected the idea that purpose is reserved for a select few. They became the women that the world was calling them to be.

You Don't Need a Dollar—You Just Need a Plan

Brandon and I have a standing date every Friday night. We don't go anywhere fancy. Most of the time, we head a few miles down the road to a sushi restaurant nearby that has a modern vibe and an outside patio. On this particular Friday, we had decided to return to a place across town we'd been only once before. This restaurant, too, has a small outdoor patio and a vibe of hipster-meets-sophistication when you walk in. There's no dress code, yet valet parking is the only option when you pull into the semicircular drive. Perhaps the quirkiness is exactly what we're drawn to.

As we drove down the freeway toward the restaurant, we both began to unpack our week- the good, the bad, the things we were working toward, the crazy thing our ten-year-old had said and what we wanted to do that weekend. The conversation began to dial down as I watched the sun begin to set behind the mountain in the distance.

"I was talking to a client today about you," Brandon said. I looked back toward him. "Yeah, he remembered you from a couple years back and just asked how you were doing."

"Aw, thanks for plugging me," I said. I smiled and turned my body back toward him to hear more.

"So, I told him you had a blog." He had a smile on his face, though I'm not sure if the smile was because he was proud of me or if it was that he was happy he could share my progress with someone.

I waited for him to finish that last sentence, to add to it, but he never did. *He told the guy I had a blog? Did he forget about the business coaching I was doing? Did he forget about the speaking engagements—albeit free engagements at that point—I had been doing locally?* Within a moment, I had shifted from gratitude to being offended.

"Why did you leave out the rest of it?" I asked. "The coaching and the speaking. They're all intertwined. You know that."

"But what *is* your message? That's where I get stuck," he said.

I'm not sure if my face turned red enough in that moment to match the boiling inside of me. It had been eight months since the launch of my blog. My email list had begun to grow rapidly, and my husband was (and probably still is) the lone male on the email list. He read my blogs and often told me when he really liked a certain story or angle that I took on it. I was confused. Honestly, I was hurt. *How does he read the blogs and then ask me what the message of my business is? If he hasn't been sure, then why not ask me this like eight months ago?*

In a sharper tone than I want to admit, I replied, "Are you serious right now? It's been the better part of a year. We've talked about what I'm doing. You've read some of my blogs. How are you confused?" I was already tearing up. I tend to go from zero to sixty pretty quickly, and without any intention to do so whatsoever, he had hit a nerve.

For the next several minutes, Brandon remained calm and listened as I flustered my way through explaining bits and pieces of my overall message. I jumped from the idea of many women sitting idly by and never daring to step into their purpose to discussing their need for inspiration and business coaching to help them take that very step that I knew they were afraid to take. I brought up our own two girls—them being the very reason I decided to completely change my career and set an example for never, ever walking away from what God places on your heart. I couldn't tell in those moments as I word-vomited on my husband if anything was resonating. I knew, on the one hand, that he wasn't (and never will be) my target audience. Was that the disconnect?

He put the right blinker on and pulled into the exit ramp on the freeway. I knew we were about six or seven minutes away from the restaurant. I also knew that because they had valet-only in their small entrance that I was either going to be a sobbing mess with puffy eyes and bright red cheeks when the guy opened my door or that I could try to regain my composure and avoid eye contact. I stopped trying to explain and just sat there in the passenger seat staring out the window at the tall glass buildings, one after another. Deep breath in. Exhale. Deep breath in. A tear drop flowing down the left side of my cheek. *Oh man, this valet guy is going to remember my tear-stained face once he catches a glimpse of me.*

"Steph, none of this was to upset you. I don't even know where I upset you, but clearly, I worded something wrong. I only tried to tell you that I had proudly shared your blog with someone. I love your writing. That's why I told him about it when he asked how you were doing."

It wasn't about the blog or the fact that he had neglected to mention my motivational speaking or business coaching. I had just stammered through eighteen tangents of what I believed in. And let me be the first to admit, I was all over the place. Each tangent was true. They were actual beliefs and concepts that I could speak or write on, but I was struggling to intertwine them into a small statement that summarized all of it. I felt the need to over-explain and give background information, hence the eighteen tangents, as I tried to relay my overall message.

We pulled up to the stop light. The restaurant was in view and just about a quarter mile beyond the intersection. I took another deep breath. "B, I know what my message is, but I'm struggling to put it into words. Well, actually my struggle is that I want to put it into too many words and can't really figure out how to just summarize it. I'm stuck, and when you asked me what my message was, it set me off. It set me off because I couldn't give you an easy, prepared response yet. It's just a reminder of how much further I have to go and makes me question whether I know what I'm even doing."

He pulled into the semicircular drive, and the valet guy opened the door. "Thank you," I said, careful to keep my head down as I got out and walked toward the back of the car.

Brandon grabbed my hand, and we walked toward the entrance. We were seated at our reserved table on the patio and gave our drink orders to the waitress. As she walked away, he turned and said, "Steph, I don't expect you to have all the answers. I don't expect you to make a certain amount of money. We found a way to get you out of our business so that you could pursue this. All I ask is that you have a plan. If you can't really answer the message piece yet, that's okay. But can you make a plan?"

There was no arguing that logic. The question was fair. *What was my plan? Was I going to continue blogging? Was I going to focus on speaking engagements? A book? A podcast? Why can't I do all those things? What was the big picture and what was the immediate step?* I nodded in agreement, hoping that the wheel of fortune of ideas in my head would soon stop spinning and land where I needed it to. I took a deep inhale of the fresh air outside. Confidence filled my lungs. "I can answer that. I do know what I want this to look like." He smiled because he knew the blueprint was up there in my mind. He knew how to ground me and narrow my focus.

After a few minutes on my soapbox as I outlined the vision of impacting women with inspiration and tangible steps for them to navigate their abundance of expectations as a wife, mother, and entrepreneur, Brandon pointed out what we both knew deep inside. "You have the big picture, but I'm not sure that what you're doing right now is how you're going to get there. There's a pivot you need to make. Nothing you've done this far is a waste. It's just been part of the journey. But it's time for the next step if you're going to make this impact with women. Do you know what that step is?"

"I know," I said, nodding, "I've been pushing it off and afraid that I didn't have the credibility, but I do. I truly believe the last ten years are the expertise no classroom could've ever taught me."

"I agree one hundred percent."

I began to fidget in my chair as I looked down at the white tablecloth, thoughts swirling through my mind. Months prior, I knew my purpose was to reach female entrepreneurs and working mamas who are struggling to blend society's expectations of them with the purpose echoing in their hearts. The blog was a start, but it wasn't enough. The small local speaking engagements were a start, but they weren't enough either.

Though I knew deep inside that a shift in my approach was necessary, I needed someone on the outside to nudge me. I had to change direction.

"If you could grab every woman by the shoulders and look her in the eye, what would you tell her?" he asked.

"That she's living below her potential. That she is uniquely qualified for a specific purpose. That she's settling right now and she doesn't have to," I started. "That we can't shape this next generation if we aren't the living, breathing example of exactly what it means to pursue a life of purpose.

That there's an actual way to create a business or project around it to serve those she's meant to impact."

I looked over at Brandon. He was taking a drink of his iced tea, but his eyes were smiling as he listened to me.

"So, what's the plan now, Steph?" he asked.

"It's time to write a book."

Chapter Takeaway

Oftentimes, the scariest step for you to take is the one that will have the biggest impact. You've worked through each chapter reframing your mindset, identifying your unique abilities, creating productivity routines, and narrowing in on your purpose. If you still feel unsure as to whether or not you have identified your actual purpose, then you are not alone. The inability to see the entire picture and purpose all at once will cause you to second-guess if you're fooling yourself or not. You aren't fooling yourself. Oftentimes, you will only see part of the picture. One or two steps at a time.

Who you are today, in this moment, is not the same woman you'll be six months or a year from now. From the day you begin to lean into that purpose, you will grow. Your character will be molded. Your resilience will be tested and strengthened. Your story will begin.

Today, in this moment, my purpose is _____.

The day(s) and time of day that I will dedicate to pursuing this passion project or business are _____.

My first step is _____.

Acknowledgments

To my husband, Brandon, for being the unwavering sense of calm in this journey and such an integral part of bringing this book to life. Thank you for embracing this vision, asking the tough questions, and walking alongside me to support it at every turn.

Printed in the United States
by Baker & Taylor Publisher Services